ENDOR⟨

These concepts of our self-image are thought provoking, and Dr. Fola-Alade presents them with refreshing energy and passion. This dynamic Pastor has something important to say about the power of ordinary people with an extraordinary vision of who they really are.

Ted Haggard
Senior Pastor of New Life Church, Colorado Springs and author of Primary Purpose & The Life-giving church.

Under his dynamic ministry Dr Fola-Alade's church has experienced dramatic growth and now this ministry is being extended through the printed word. His second book So who do you think you really are? is packed with helpful insights and is a must for all who want to grow in effective Christian living.

Colin Dye
Senior Pastor of Kensington Temple, and Leader of the London City Church Network.

This is an extremely insightful book. If you can really grasp Dr Sola's message and the sentiments contained therein, I have no doubt that your life will be totally transformed. The book is packed with spiritual nuggets and truths. Dr Sola skillfully brings the reader to a point of self-reflection, so much so that it is inevitable that you will be unable to avoid the soul-searching question presented in the book's title, So, who do you really think you are? This is a book that must be read.

Bishop John Francis
Overseer and Founder of Ruach Ministries,
London, United Kingdom.

My friend, Sola Fola-Alade is one of hundreds of Nigerian pastors planting churches that are quickly becoming the largest and most significant churches in various countries in which they are planted. He is a dynamic young visionary who is committed to discipling a genre of leaders who will have significant impact in their spheres of influence. Sola is a breadth of air amidst a stream of ministry that is stagnated in tradition. He writes from his passion, with great clarity and insight. No doubt we will be hearing his name spoken in many established circles of ministry.

Joseph Thompson

An Associate Pastor at New Life Church in Colorado Springs, CO, USA, with Senior Pastor Ted Haggard. He is also the founder of Yeshua Ministries.

SO, WHO DO YOU
REALLY
THINK
YOU ARE?

SO, WHO DO YOU
REALLY
THINK
YOU ARE?

DR. SOLA FOLA-ALADE MB;BS

VISION MEDIA COMMUNICATIONS

So, Who Do You Really Think You Are?
Copyright © 2003 by Dr Sola Fola-Alade
Reprint 2005

Published by
Vision Media Communications
The Leadership Centre
1 Warton Road
London
E15 2LA
www.developingleaders.net

All Scriptures, unless otherwise stated, are from the Holy Bible,
New International Version. Copyright © 1973, 1978, 1984 by
International Bible Society. Used by permission.

ISBN 0 9539796 1 X

Printed in the United Kingdom.

ACKNOWLEDGEMENTS

I would like to say a big 'Thank you' to God for choosing and using me. He shone His light in and through me, in order to bring the knowledge of His love and will to a hurting generation.

And to all the members of *Trinity Chapel*. You respond positively to God's words through His servant. You are indeed a people being prepared for a prepared place.

And to my writing consultants and editors Pat Walker, Tokunbo Emmanuel and David Porter. God has used you in articulating the thoughts in my heart in a way that is readable and understandable.

A big thank you to my wife for once again releasing me to do what God has called me to do.

And to my two lovely sons, Toni and Tola. You are both my greatest investment and my favourite teachers. You have taught me the joy of fathering.

You are my very first 'sheep'. Thank you for releasing me to be a shepherd to others.

CONTENTS

DEDICATED TO...

My Wife

You are indeed a chosen treasure. My best friend and my most trusted confidante. My cheerleader and the one to whom God has entrusted the care and nurture of my tender heart. Thank you for believing in me.

My Father

For raising me with the best that money could not buy. You built my confidence by giving us the best - laughter, joy, hope, moderation, discipline, exposure and experience. You gave us as loving and secure a home as you could, in the absence of my late mother. Thank you.

My Brothers and Sisters

Who have nurtured, encouraged and accommodated their 'baby brother' in his many endeavours.

My Late Mother

Thank you for the unconditional love and generosity you demonstrated in the seven years that I knew you. Your blessed memory remains with me forever.

My Two Wonderful Sons

*Who are the promise of a brighter future,
the potential for a finer tomorrow and the hope of
the next generation. This book is written to preserve
and protect people just like you.*

FOREWORD

The greatest discovery in life is the discovery of one-self. Until we know who we are we will never live a full and fulfilled life. It is a fact that we see the world through our perception of ourselves. Our picture of ourselves determines the picture we have of others. Psychologists and behavioural scientists have long believed that most human interpersonal problems stem from a poor self-image, low self-esteem, and a low self-worth. These three components of the human entity are the keys to how we relate to ourselves and how we interpret life. Everything hangs on our self-picture.

Nothing can substitute for a good healthy self-image, high self-esteem and a strong self-worth. These three determine our success in relationships, marriage, business, society and life as a whole. A reference to the priority to be given to the values of self-love and self-concept is found in an encounter between the great Jewish rabbi, Jesus Christ, and a rich young man who asked a pertinent question: 'What is the most important commandment in the law of God?' The answer given by Jesus has not been fully understood: 'Love the Lord your God with all your heart, soul, mind and your strength and love your neighbour as yourself'. Many have interpreted this answer to mean love God and love your neighbour. But I wish to note that emphasis of Jesus is placed on loving God and loving self, stressing that you can only love your neighbour to the same degree that you love yourself. In essence it is more important to love yourself than to attempt to love your neighbour. The value you place on others can be no greater than you place on yourself. The principle is essential to understand if we are to live a life of confidence, fulfilment and freedom.

Dr Sola Fola Alade in this book has taken a much needed issue that is in desperate demand in our cold, friendless, self-seeking, self-centred, dysfunctional societies. The evidence of self-hatred, low self-worth and poor self-image is manifested in our nation's self-destructive behaviour. The continual rise of suicides, lack of effective conflict resolution, and frustrated relationships are the loud cries of the hidden pain deep in the soul of mankind for a revelation of his self-worth and meaning in life. This work is a tremendous contribution to the unending search for significance. Dr Sola, in both a simple yet profound way, unmasks the hidden fears of our hearts, defines our hurts, charts the history of our journey to date and presents practical, relevant and sound biblical answers to the questions of the human heart. This book is a must for all who want to discover the truth about themselves and strive to become their best.

I highly recommend this book to old and young alike and know it will become a reference for years in your libraries. I challenge you to peel the wisdom from these pages and let the time-tested truth hidden between the covers of this work help you embrace the real beauty of who you really are.

Dr Myles Munroe
Bahamas Faith Ministries International
Nassau, Bahamas

PREFACE

One of the major plagues of our generation is a confusion of identity - a sense of uncertainty as to who we really are. This condition manifests itself in a number of ways:

A poor self-concept — when you think you are not good enough;

Insecurities — when you are not confident in who you are;

Inferiority complex — when you consider yourself substandard to others.

This dysfunction is the result of damages to human personality in a person's formative and developmental years.

Most of the dysfunctional behaviour we have to deal with in adulthood is the consequence of exposure to events that we could not cope with at some critical stage in our development. These traumas paralyse the mind and leave us crippled in the area of our emotions to the point where we are unable to function in a 'normal' capacity in life.

Many have been adversely affected by past circumstances and cannot relate appropriately to others. This is the reason why many marriages are breaking up today.

Handicaps in the mind leave us feeling somewhat incompetent in the various positions we hold in society. Many settle for mediocrity and remain under-achievers in life. No wonder that many struggle with depression, nervous breakdowns and suicidal tendencies.

In order to overcome these negative trends, we need to address the question *'Who do you really think you are?'* This book is an attempt to tackle this question and provide hope to many who have been bruised.

INTRODUCTION

'THE SILENT KILLER'

Over the past few centuries the world has seen masses of people wiped out as a result of devastating natural disasters. Earthquakes, floods, hurricanes and volcanic eruptions have claimed whole cities and nations, and we have seen entire tribes and communities obliterated by starvation, war and disease.

From about the 14th to the 17th century, the Bubonic Plague raged all over Europe. Homes were torn apart and families were forced to watch helplessly while their loved ones suffered and died in agony.

In the 20th century, malnutrition surfaced as the faceless assassin in many developing nations. For a while, the West looked on as the health and strength of thousands in the Third World gradually diminished. Emaciated bodies and skeletal corpses lined dusty streets, while the barrier of a television screen safely shielded us from the question, *'Am I my brother's keeper?'*

Today, in the 21st century, surprising as it may seem, one can almost say that *rejection* is the new lethal epidemic silently destroying many lives. It is a silent killer because, unlike physical trauma, the pain and injury can lie undetected for many years and then become infected and complicated until it is potentially fatal.

THE STARVATION OF LOVE

It is evident that modern society is beleaguered with wounds, pain and frustration. With the advent of the credit card and automatic money transfer, we are not only tending towards a 'cashless society' but are also living in a 'loveless society'. The pace of life has increased astronomically and the sense of community has been sacrificed for individualism.

Everyone has a need to be loved and to love in return but for some bizarre reason, there does not seem to be enough love in the world today. Mother Teresa said, 'The biggest disease today is not leprosy or tuberculosis, but rather the feeling of being deserted, neither wanted nor cared for by anybody.'

Love and affection are as crucial to humans as water and sunlight are to plants. At the beginning of life, every individual is somewhat like a plant whose buds are green, yet closed. It has all the promise of colour and beauty, but is still in incubation. Only when the bud of a flower is refreshed with water and receives the warmth of sunlight, coupled with nourishment from the mothering soil, will it grow, unfold and expose all the latent beauty that it has hidden inside.

Likewise the human soul. From the beginning of life we must receive the warmth of human love and assurance if we are to blossom and expose the unique beauty and talent that God has placed within each and every one.

DEVELOPMENT OF HUMAN PERSONALITY

'Even a child is known by his actions, by whether his conduct is pure and right.' (Proverbs 20:11)

It amazes me to see how my older son has grown over the past few years. I still remember seeing him as a tiny collection of tissue with a heartbeat on the ultrasound monitor. My wife and I were fascinated by the tiny weeks-old heart beating on the screen. I can recollect to this day the look on his face when he was born.

EVERYONE HAS A NEED TO BE LOVED AND TO LOVE IN RETURN BUT FOR SOME BIZARRE REASON, THERE DOES NOT SEEM TO BE ENOUGH LOVE IN THE WORLD TODAY.

Now that he is four years old, I am full of awesome wonder at how his personality has flourished into that of a curious, assertive, compassionate and expressive young man. One can earnestly say that if he is nurtured and cultivated in a loving and secure environment, this child holds the promise of becoming a confident, charismatic leader of his generation. The observation of my children's conception, birth and development proves to me that an intelligent being must be behind the creation of this entire universe and everything within it.

Personality can be defined as the social manifestation or expression of an individual. It is this expression that distinguishes one from another, and characterises one's unique contribution to society. It is that very expression which adds a different note, melody or tune to the orchestra of community. A damaged instrument will taint the music of the whole ensemble, just as hostile forces injuring the bud of a flower will prevent it from blooming.

More so with a human being who does not receive the vital ingredients of love in the form of attention, affection, assurance, security and praise. He or she will remain closed-in, and is likely to wither in that state, never manifesting the expression of their true worth. This world will never discover the unique fragrance their personality would have brought to this universe. What a shame!

Many people have been raised under harsh and hostile conditions without the love that is required for them to blossom to full fruition. They have been brought up under adverse, insecure and life-threatening conditions, hence they are often bitter, angry and in pain.

Small wonder we have so many people with behavioural problems and many others who are frustrated and angry at society. According to statistics, patients with mental problems occupy two-thirds of all hospital beds in the USA; suicide is the highest killer of people between the ages of 18 and 21 years old; 70% of all juveniles in state reform institutions come from father-less homes and 50-60% of young people in America grow up in single parent homes.

THE ENEMY IS AFTER OUR CHILDREN

Half of today's young people have lived through the divorce of their parents. 63% of young people live in households in which both parents work outside the home. 77% of teenagers say their mothers are hardly ever home when they return from school. 98% of teen-agers spend over 11 hours per week watching television.

Satan is very aware of the great potential that resides in our children. He is not oblivious to the treasure and gift that God has deposited in each child. He knows that if these children grow up in wholesome, loving environments they will become a major threat to his kingdom. Hence his arsenal is always aimed at damaging and destroying children. His strategy is to deprive them of the love, security and nurturing environment required for their proper development. He launches his attacks on individuals at all stages of life, as they journey from the womb to the tomb.

How can we counteract this devilish scheme that is threatening the sanity of the coming generation? Is there any provision in Scripture for the reversal of this down-ward trend?

References

Stringer, Doug. The Fatherless Generation (Hope For a Generation in Search For Identity): *Shippensburg, Destiny Image, 1995.*

McDowell, Josh. The Disconnected Generation (Saving Our Youth From Self-Destruction): *Nashville, Word Publishing, 2000.*

PART ONE

THE PERSON

Chapter 1

DO YOU KNOW WHO YOU ARE?

There is one thing that spans the whole of society, regardless of colour, class or creed: the quest for self-knowledge. Every one asks the question 'Who am I, really?' This is an age-old question that probably dates as far back as the Garden of Eden.

Another question we ask is '*How* am I?' in the sense that we want to know how we are rated by others. This, I believe, is a question that has become even more important in this 'designer label' age with its concern for image projection. Regardless of how the questions are asked, it is obvious we live in a generation that is confused about identity. Oblivious of our uniqueness, we strive tirelessly to be or look like someone else. Worse still, we spend half of our lives trying to prove we are somebody when we are not really sure of ourselves.

If you do not comprehend who you are or where you are from, you may spend an entire lifetime wondering what you are good at and where you will end up. Your identity affects your destiny.

MIRROR, MIRROR ON THE WALL

We do not believe what our own mirror tells us. We tend to exaggerate or eliminate what we see when we stand in front of it. We ask our mirrors, like the wicked old witch in the fairy tale, 'Mirror, mirror on the wall who is the fairest of them all?' Inwardly, we dread the mirror's answer. 'Would it be Snow White — or Winter Grey?'

When we stand in front of our mirrors, we tend not to appreciate ourselves, but rather to compare ourselves with others.

IF YOU DO NOT COMPREHEND WHO YOU ARE OR WHERE YOU ARE FROM, YOU MAY SPEND AN ENTIRE LIFETIME WONDERING WHAT YOU ARE GOOD AT AND WHERE YOU WILL END UP. YOUR IDENTITY AFFECTS YOUR DESTINY.

Many people struggle with the way they see themselves. Their perception is further amplified by the shortcomings or failures they experience in life. Some people wrestle with issues they dare not discuss in public. Others try to cover up insecurities with the clothes they wear. They reason, 'If I can just "dress-up", people will not realise how shabby I feel on the inside.' It is imperative for success and fulfilment in life that we address and overcome any unhealthy self-perception.

'Who can tell me who I really am?' This generation begs for an answer. By now we should know that the mirror does not give the answer. A man cannot be a true mirror unto himself.

PLEASE TELL ME WHO I AM!

Unable to get an answer from the mirror, we turn to other people to 'mirror' us. Directly or indirectly, we seek their opinion for affirmation and validation. We ask others how we look, how we smell, how we behave and so on. Even when the question is not articulated, they still get the message. A stance, an expression, a posture, a tone of voice, these can all be signals in a net-work of silent clues working together to elicit the approval that we so desperately crave.

If someone is asked to perform a song, give a presentation or propose a toast, it is not unusual to hear the quiet enquiry afterwards, 'How did I do?'. When a person is introduced at a party, he may laugh at the jokes being told, politely respond when asked questions and join the general conversation, but underneath he feels totally self-conscious. As soon as the party is over he asks a friend, 'So what do you think they thought of me?'

We probably have not stopped to consider that in seeking other people's opinions, we are submitting our lives and destinies to their judgement. We take their assessment seriously and begin to live by it. If, for example, someone who has formed a negative opinion about us conveys his feelings without reservation, we may allow it to shape our behaviour. Whether instantly or gradually, we begin to behave as if the negative report were true.

JESUS KNEW WHO HE WAS

Jesus did not entrust His destiny to man's judgement. When He asked His disciples who men were saying He was (Matthew 16:13), it was not for the sake of validation. He was not seeking men's approval. He was asking this question to see whether the disciples themselves knew who He *really* was. It is possible to relate to and even live with someone without knowing the person. Even your spouse, the person with whom you share your most intimate moments, can never know you completely.

IT IS IMPERATIVE FOR SUCCESS AND FULFILMENT IN LIFE THAT WE ADDRESS AND OVERCOME ANY UNHEALTHY SELF-PERCEPTION.

Only God knows and understands you. He is aware of the changes you go through from time to time. God appreciates your idiosyncrasies and habits, your individuality and the things that make you different from others. He loves you for who you are. It takes a discerning person to perceive you through God's eyes. Most of the time, people will judge you wrongly — just as the crowd misjudged Jesus' true identity. It is more important for you to know yourself accurately than for you to know what people think of you.

IN SEEKING OTHER PEOPLE'S OPINIONS, WE ARE SUBMITTING OUR LIVES AND DESTINIES TO THEIR JUDGEMENT.

WHAT'S THE DIFFERENCE?

In order to discover ourselves, we need to explore the differences between who we think we are, who others think we are, and our true identity.

Who We Think We Are (Self-Perception)

As noted earlier, self-image has to do with the way we see ourselves. Everyone person has an image of himself or herself that may or may not be true. Most times we do not have the precise or accurate picture. Either we have one that is higher than ourselves and are called arrogant, or one that is lower than ourselves and are called timid. In many ways, both views are untrue.

What we sometimes refer to as 'humility' is not a true image of how God sees us. We often consider ourselves

'a good-for-nothing sinner', and even if we do not verbalise it, we constantly rehearse it in our minds. This breeds
a lack of confidence and feelings of inadequacy which are
not attributes from God. They are lies that need to be
flushed from our minds with the Word of God.

Taking a pompous stand about oneself is equally erro-
neous. We are told not to think of ourselves more highly
than we ought (Romans 12:3). Hype and gloss are not
God's way. We need to see ourselves in line with the
Word of God.

Who Others Think You Are (People's opinion)

Someone once recalled that while she was growing
up, her older brother and others around her teased her
mercilessly. They called her 'Big-head!'. The truth is, a
growing child's head is sometimes slightly oversized, because the rest of the body does not develop as quickly.
This makes the head seem out of proportion for a little
while. Even after the rest of her body eventually meas-
ured up, she retained the perception that her head was
larger by comparison.

She grew to be so self-conscious that when anybody
became attracted to her and called her beautiful, she
would insist, 'How can I be beautiful, my head is far too
big!'

People will always have an opinion about you
based on their perceptions and prejudices. Whether you
believe it or not is up to you. Unfortunately, most peo-

ple spend a lot of their time ruminating on negative opinions held by others. It is no wonder that a lot of people in the world are struggling with low self-esteem.

Who God Thinks We Are (True Identity)

Your true identity is how God sees you; not what others see in you or what you see in yourself. He knows who you really are and is not influenced by your self-perception or people's opinion.

Much of God's work in our lives is to bring us into an accurate understanding of who we are in Him. He longs to liberate us from the bondage of negative perceptions and unveil the real person He created us to be. The process of deliverance starts, I believe, with an understanding of the concepts of 'self'.

Chapter 2

HOW DID WE BECOME
SELF-CONSCIOUS?

O ne thought that has constantly puzzled philosophers for many centuries is the concept of 'Self'. It is generally understood that human beings are unique compared to all other living creatures. René Descartes is often quoted as having said that our ability to think or reflect is what gives us the sense of being. 'I think, therefore I am'. By this, one can deduce that things that do not have the power of thought, (i.e. a mind), are not aware of their existence. Other mammals such as monkeys or dolphins are very intelligent creatures possessing mind-boggling memories, yet their sense of 'self' cannot be compared to that of humans. Human beings do not only have the capacity to be aware of their existence, but also have the ability to place a worth or value on themselves.

THE BEGINNING OF CONSCIOUSNESS

God made this possible when He created man in the be-ginning, as documented in Genesis 2:7.

'The LORD God formed the man from the dust of the ground and breathed into his nostrils the breath of life and the man became a living being.'

Man was essentially created from the major components of dust or earth. God moulded man from the ground, and gave life to him by breathing His spirit into him.

This creation process meant that man was able to access his physical world via the body's five senses (touch, sight, hearing, smell and taste). Through his spirit he is able to perceive and communicate with the spiritual world, the main channels of communication being prayer, dreams, visions, intuition etc. The part of man that 'came alive' during creation is the faculty by which he relates to himself and others. Hence man is a fully functioning social being, as well as a physical and spiritual one.

WHAT IS SELF-CONCEPT?

Self-concept is simply the philosophy behind understanding one's self. It is gained from the various ways in which we see, feel and understand ourselves. It is the system of beliefs that define what we think about ourselves. There are a number of things that make up what is today termed 'self-concept'.

Self-Image. This has to do with how we *see* ourselves. For example, a man may consider himself a confident person or the clumsy type.

Self-Esteem. How we *feel* about ourselves. For example the person lacking confidence will probably have negative or untoward feelings about himself.

Self-Worth. This has to do with how we *value* ourselves. For example the sense and feeling of a lack of confidence usually derives from not placing the right value or worth upon one's self.

These concepts are not necessarily real, but perceived. They are not subject to any form of scientific testing, but are relative to the person doing the perceiving. As the saying goes 'Beauty is in the eye of the beholder.'

It is who we think we are that we will eventually become. Hence, we are the final judges of our own worth and value, as well as the image we perceive of ourselves. Other 'beholders' may not necessarily judge us favourably or fairly, but our judgement must be positive if we are to succeed in our undertakings.

'For as he thinketh in his heart, so is he.' (Proverbs. 23:7 KJV).

Descartes' words, 'I think therefore I am', align with the above-stated wisdom from the Holy Bible. A man is basically who he thinks he is. He becomes what he currently believes himself to be, and whatever he continuously thinks of and says to himself, he will eventually become. The equation has a little more complexity than this, but in its essence, the underlying philosophy holds true. Whatever data or information is fed through the mind will ultimately affect self-concept.

IT IS WHO WE THINK WE ARE THAT WE WILL EVENTUALLY BECOME. HENCE, WE ARE THE FINAL JUDGES OF OUR OWN WORTH AND VALUE.

NATURE AND NURTURE

To further understand man's self-consciousness and how the human personality is shaped, two main factors need to be considered. The first of these can be described as *natural factors*, which are innate to a child from before birth. Every child has a unique personality and different social, behavioural and emotional disposition. Before we were ever formed, God created us to be unique. Another natural factor that determines our personality traits and behavioural inclinations is our genetic make-up. This comprises a familiar pattern that is handed down from generation to generation.

The other major factor determining how we eventually see and feel about ourselves is the *nurture factor*. 'Nurture' has to do with the environment, that is, the social, emotional, physical and spiritual circumstances in which we are raised. It has to do with whether a person has been loved or unloved, accepted or unaccepted. It also has to do with the amount and quality of attention he or she received while growing up. Invariably, we see ourselves in the light of whatever was consistently fed into the computer of our minds.

I personally believe that 'nurture' rather than 'nature' is a stronger determinant of how a person eventually perceives himself or herself. Even though a seed, for instance, has the inherent potential to become a beautiful, colourful plant with radiant flowers, if it is not given adequate water, soil and sunlight it will never grow to be (or see itself as) the beautiful flower it was meant to be.

SECURITY AND SIGNIFICANCE.

In his book on *The Sense of Who We Are*, Selwyn Hughes suggests that our 'identity' depends on three main things. One's sense of *security* stems from having had the feeling of being unconditionally loved; one's sense of *self-worth* derives from having been valued; finally, one's sense of *significance* is a result of having had a feeling of meaning and purpose.

Hughes states that these three basic needs can only be fully met through a genuine relationship with God, but if parents were to love their children deeply, and were to instil in them a sense of belonging, they would grow up having a sense of *security*.

What is more, if parents were to train their children to make an impact upon their world by directing them towards the expression of their own uniqueness and innate abilities, then their children would enjoy a deeper feeling of *significance*. If children were to see in the eyes of their parents, an admiration and esteem for them as important individuals, they would develop a healthy sense of *self-worth*.

'I AM NOT WHAT I THINK I AM; I AM NOT WHAT YOU THINK I AM. I AM WHAT I THINK THAT YOU THINK I AM.'

Of these three basic needs, it is a child's *self-worth* that is most responsible for how he or she esteems himself or herself. If one is tempted to dismiss the subtle difference between being loved and being valued, one is at the same time suggesting that there is no difference between the need to be cherished and the need to know that we are worthwhile people. Seeing how worthwhile we are in someone else's eyes contributes greatly to our sense of self-worth.

Hughes' conclusions during his study of adolescent psychology nicely summarises this issue of self-worth and self-image:

> 'I am not what I think I am; I am not what you think I am. I am what I think that you think I am.'

In other words, a child comes to sense how much he is valued, not by what his parents (or those responsible for his nurture) think, but by what he thinks they think of him. This truth alone accounts for the negative self-perceptions held by most people.

References

Hughes, Selwyn. Christ empowered living (Celebrating your significance in God), *Nashville, Broadman & Hollman, 2001.*

PART TWO

THE PROBLEM

Chapter 3
SYMPTOMS & SIGNS
OF A POOR SELF-IMAGE

In medicine, symptoms are the things patients complain about but signs are the things the doctor can see. They lead doctors to where the real problem is. The following symptoms and signs are results of a root problem — poor self-image. We may have suffered or may still be suffering from these things in varying degrees.

A Critical Spirit

Have you ever been around someone who is always critical of other people? This is a sign of a poor self-image. You mention somebody's success or compliment someone in their presence, and say, 'Ah, *that* lady, oh...' Then they begin to tell you what they know she's *really* like.

If you went to a conference with a person with a poor self-image, they wouldn't say they found it enjoyable. They would say something like, 'It was OK, but did you see the speaker's suit? That suit has some big, ugly bold stripes. That is, belittling the speaker's image because they just cannot stand others having a better image than they have themselves.

Love for Position

People with a poor self-image will jockey for position. They will tell you that they cannot do the job unless you give them the title of Vice So-and-So, Senior Manager, or Director. Then when they get there they do not accomplish anything! All they do is look around for whoever wants to take their position and they are ready to push them down. These people are so devoid of power that they need the title of the position to give them significance. It is a symptom to look out for.

Self-Criticism

Sufferers from a poor self-image express feelings of self-hatred. Listen to them closely enough and you will realise that they hate themselves. Such people are constantly expressing feelings of rejection.

Excessive shyness

After preaching a series of messages on the topic of self-image, I felt it necessary to introduce the study in our church's weekly home worship groups. Shortly afterwards, I received an email from a member of the church that confirmed the timeliness of the studies.

The gentleman told me that something came up during the weekly home meetings he hosts in his home. It was an issue regarding his own battle with self-esteem. Up until then, whenever a meeting in his home had finished, most of the people went straight home immediately afterwards. However, when people in the group began to share their personal concerns regarding the way they felt about themselves, he took the opportunity to disclose his own insecurities admitting that he was extremely shy. This was the reason he always appeared reserved. This led to further discussion and it came to light that the other people who had been coming to his home for the weekly meetings had not realised that he was shy. From then on, he was able to relax more with the group and there was more warmth in the atmosphere in his future meetings. Excessive shyness is a symptom to look out for.

Over-dressing

Many are fond of using clothes to cover up their problems. They dress up to hide what is inside them. Clothes are sometimes statements that we belong to a certain class. Designer shoes and ties can camouflage, but none of them can ever take away feelings of inferiority that reside within the soul.

'Did you Mean that as a Compliment?'

People who have low self-esteem find it hard to accept compliments paid to them. If you were to say, 'That dress looks lovely on you', they would say something like, 'What, this old thing? I bought it in the sale at half price!' They are eager to give you the feeling that they are just a filthy piece of rag that does not really have the right to wear anything decent.

The other day I was in a minicab being driven by a lady driver. She was driving a Mercedes and I said 'This is a nice car.' She shrugged her shoulders and said in a very humble voice 'Well, it gets me from A to B.' I felt like saying, 'Well, if you just want a car that gets you from A to B then step out, take my car and give me yours in exchange!'

The Name-Dropping Syndrome

Some people are constantly trying to hide behind something or someone. Serial name-droppers need to be associated with someone they consider better than themselves. They will intimate to anyone who will listen that they are in close contact with a well-to-do or famous person, their pastor or someone of significance in the hierarchy of their organisation. They do not feel important enough in themselves so they pester and hang around these kinds of people in order to be associated with their importance. They 'hob-nob' with popular people because they need other peoples' images to 'prop' them up.

Competitive Spirit

People who are into competition and rivalry also display signs of insecurity. If their next-door neighbour moves to a bigger house in a better area, they feel the need to show that they can do the same. Within a short time, they move their family to a better area before they can afford to do so. They will mortgage themselves up to their eyeballs and struggle to keep up the payments just to boast of a larger house. If their sibling buys a new car, they must get a newer, faster, bigger car and parade it all over town.

It even spills over into churches. One pastor buys a building for his congregation and the insecure pastor, seeing this, forces his congregation to support his desire for a bigger building. It will not be too long before such a church closes down.

Boastfulness

People who feel the need to brag and boast may also be covering an insecurity problem. Conceited conduct and activities that result in an overt or subtle 'put-down' usually stem from an inner conflict. Some people love to lord their success over others. They use their good fortune as a tool to belittle you and speak down at you. This is a classic case of someone with no real security within him or herself, who uses the money, position or status as a podium for condescending arrogance.

Racist Mentality

I once took a look at some of the factors that promote racism and it occurred to me that the problem was at least two-fold. Firstly, people in certain organisations and positions have held onto a certain image of people of colour. Some are still of the mentality that people of colour are somehow 'less' than other people. Whether or not they vocalise it, they feel that power ought only to be shared among people who belong to an élite club.

The other factor is that people of colour still limit themselves to certain positions. They cannot see themselves beyond certain levels. Though they may verbalise their desire for those positions and may even attempt to apply for a prestigious job in the 'city', there seems to be something blocking them from entering their destiny. This is a bad symptom of a low self-esteem and the following story explains why.

A while ago, an experiment was carried out with the flesh-eating fish, piranha. These fish are generally slow, but they eat their live prey very swiftly. A piranha was placed into an aquarium with goldfish in it. Within a short while all the goldfish had been devoured. Those who were carrying out the experiment wanted to devise a way in which both the goldfish and the piranha could be housed together within the same aquarium. They placed the piranha inside a clear glass bowl within the aquarium creating a barrier between the piranha and the goldfish. The piranha swam around inside the bowl, and any time it tried to swim towards any of the other goldfish to eat them, it hit its head on the side of the bowl. This went on for quite a while until the piranha realised that if it tried to go after the goldfish, it would end up hitting its head against the glass bowl and so before long, it just stopped trying.

Afterwards, the bowl was subtly removed, leaving the piranha in the aquarium. It was discovered that the piranha no longer attempted to eat the goldfish. It had been conditioned against trying, having hit its head on the glass far too many times in the past. The piranha had created a mental boundary as though the glass restraining it was still in position.

It is possible that the government and certain levels of senior management have removed the glass ceilings that have been preventing people from advancing in the past. It is possible that the invisible doors have now been taken away. The problem is that, because people have been hitting their heads for so many years on rejected applications, like the piranha, they have conditioned themselves against continuing to try. They have conditioned themselves against going beyond the levels to which they have become accustomed. With a renewed self-image through God's word, nothing will stand in the way of our becoming all God intended for us to become.

All the above are symptoms and signs of a poor self-image. The list, however, is not exhaustive. The next chapter explains how the root of these manifestations are linked to happenings in our past.

Chapter 4
BEHIND THE VEIL
OF YOUR PAST

T he person we are today is a sum total of all our past experiences to date. We are basically a product of all the things we have passed through in life. Actions and incidents that we have been exposed to, whether good or bad, leave indelible marks upon our lives.

It is said that the girl is the mother of the woman. This implies that the experiences and environment to which a little girl is exposed will determine her perspective, disposition, fears, reactions and responses in adult years. For instance, a girl who did not know the warm, secure, assuring love of a father while growing up, and who later was sexually abused by an uncle in her teenage years, will more than likely despise and rebel against all male authority in her adult years. She will probably be fiercely independent, hostile, defensive and abrasive. She will probably be withdrawn and cold in her relationships and may not be capable of being fully trusting or intimate in her adult relationships, especially within the marital context.

In his book on inner healing, Dr David A. Seamands explains that the inner child of the past could be so fearful, defeated and self-displeasing that no matter what she wants to do, she just can not make friends or speak out. When she has an opinion to express or a heavy responsibility to handle, she (the wounded girl) may keep her (the adult woman) from becoming the person she was born to be. This is a classic scenario where the past can rob us of our future.

Negative experiences reinforce a negative self-image. However, there is much benefit in revisiting them with the redemptive power of the cross. The following factors that affect self-image are crucial for the emancipation of a caged personality.

Family Environment

Parental influence is one of the major causes of a poor self-image. Negative words continuously spoken into the life of a person can cause them to have a reduced opinion of themselves. Many of us have grown up under much negativity. The constant negative words we hear about ourselves, especially from parents or extended family members, tend to stick.

For a long time I faced this predicament. Being the last child in my family, and coming from a cultural background that expects the youngest child to do most of the work in the house, I constantly rebelled against what I felt was an unfair system. If there was something to be done in the house, some unpleasant household chore, nobody did it. All eyes were on me as the one who had to get it done.

I liked to spend a lot of time by myself, reading in particular, so when I was called upon to do things I usually responded slowly. After observing my reluctance over a period, members of my family began to say, 'Sola, you are lazy. You are very lazy.' Hearing this over and over again convinced me that I was truly a lazy boy! It was not until I saw the need to consciously reject this stereotype that I began to experience liberation. I did not want it to limit me as a person.

Your Environment

What our parents do, or don't do, to us can also affect us. I came into possession of an old poem that stirred me when I first read it, and still rings true today:

If a child lives with criticism, he learns to condemn,

If a child lives with hostility, he learns to fight,

If a child lives with ridicule, he learns to be shy,

If a child lives with shame, he learns to feel guilty.

If a child lives with tolerance, he learns to be patient,

If a child lives with encouragement he learns self-confidence,

If a child lives with praise, he learns to appreciate,

If a child lives with fairness, he learns justice,

If a child lives with security, he learns to have faith,

If a child lives with approval, he learns to like himself.

If a child lives with acceptance and friendship, he learns to find love in the world.

Parental influence, or the influence of other people with authority over us during our formative years, has a very powerful impact upon our lives. If, for example, your parents were fond of embarrassing you in public, unless you take active steps to overcome those memories you will always feel ashamed and embarrassed when asked to appear in public.

I was blessed to have been raised in a home where my father openly showed affection and cared for us. Hence, people say I have a very optimistic, friendly and trusting view of the world and other people.

Sibling Rivalry

When parents show more love and favouritism to one child than to the others, they set them up against each other. The less-favoured children are always trying to work extra hard to gain the same kind of affection that the favourite is receiving from their parents. What happens in the end is that the ones who are craving affection go to the other extreme and begin to seek negative attention. They will become aggressive and disruptive, or start behaving badly at school (whatever it takes to get their parents to notice them). It drives the siblings apart and often causes devastating effects in adult life. This could easily have been avoided with the use of better parenting skills.

Negative Words

As parents we must be careful of what we say around our children. I know a certain woman who accompanied her son to his school in order to have a word with his teachers. She asked if they would help him overcome his slowness. As noble as this may be, she said it in front of the boy. From that moment on, the child grew up with those words ringing in his ears: 'I am slow. I will always need help because I am very slow.' The parents wonder to this day why their child is not doing well. When they chastise him, all he says in his puzzled response is, 'But I am slow!'

Lack of Affirmation

Perhaps you missed your child's school play. You did not consider it important enough for prioritisation. All the other parents were there, clapping for their children, but you were conspicuously absent. Your son or daughter may have played the role of a donkey. He does not have to be the star of the play. But think twice before you decide against supporting him or her.

I asked my parents to come and watch my school play 'Aladdin and his wonderful lamp'. It was so important to me that I asked my mother to sew the costume and re-sew it a number of times. I wanted to get it just right. I was so proud to be in this play that I invited my entire family also.

When we got to the school, it turned out, to my horror, that some other boy was playing Aladdin! They had all expected me to play the star! Well, at least they came. For those children whose parents did not come, there would be no laughter or recounting of stories of foolishness. There would be no memories of the event. Just a silence and an emptiness in the child's heart when he heard his friends talking about it in the following weeks. Sometimes our priorities have unimaginable, long-lasting results.

Bad Experiences in Life

An experiment was once performed where four monkeys were put in a cage. In the middle of the cage was a pole going upwards with bananas at the top. The more ambitious of the monkeys climbed up the pole, but were met with an electric shock when they reached the top. However, because they were hungry they kept on trying to climb this pole, only to be met again and again with electric shocks. In the end, those who had been shocked a few times stopped trying and retired to one corner of the cage.

TO USE JOHN MAXWELL'S WORDS: 'DON'T LET FAILURE MAKE A MONKEY OUT OF YOU.'

One of the monkeys was taken away and replaced with a new monkey, who did not know about the electric shocks. After a while, each time they sent in a new monkey, the others would pull him down and indicate what the perils were. 'We've been there, tried it and got the T-shirt. Electric shocks at the top, don't even try it.' The original monkeys that received the shock were eventually all removed from the cage. None of the new monkeys had ever experienced the shock themselves, but after a while, they too stared at the bananas and refused to get them for themselves. Meanwhile, the electric shock had long been removed. The monkeys just remained there, salivating, making no attempt to go for the bananas.

To use John Maxwell's words 'Don't let failure make a monkey out of you.'

Embarrassing Moments

I know of a man who, when he was around five years old, knew he was called to be a preacher. He used to tell everybody he met about the Lord and what he was learning in his Sunday school classes. He used to stand on a box in his back garden and preach to the other children in the neighbourhood. He even used to preach to the cats and the dogs whenever he got the chance. Everybody knew that he wanted to be a preacher.

On the first day he started at his new school, he was unfamiliar with his surroundings and a little afraid of the new environment. He did not know that he had to put his hand up when he wanted to go to the toilet. He tried to hold it until playtime, but he couldn't wait and he ended up making a mess in his underpants in class. The teacher saw what he had done, and for some reason decided to make a public spectacle of him. She announced to the whole class that he had wet his pants, called him a 'Dunce with a double-d', and had the whole class laughing at him. The teacher put a sign on him saying that he was a dirty boy. At playtime the other children called him 'dirty-boy' and other names, and picked on him for a long time afterwards. He never was able to live down the stigma and shame of that day.

The worst thing about the incident was that it made him lose his drive to preach. It made him quite a reserved and introverted young man, and removed his desire to speak to people or even approach anyone to tell them about the Lord. It affected his marriage and it was a long time before he regained his confidence. Through prayer and perseverance, he has now become a pastor, but the scars of the incident are still perceivable today, in his delivery and carriage.

Other People's Opinions

In my final year of training to be a medical doctor, there was a senior registrar who was a surgeon. We were on our ward round one day and questions were being asked of the medical students. I was asked how I would excise a specific affliction. I did not even get to answer the question because another student spoke and gave an incorrect answer. The registrar, however, pointed to me and said, 'You are a failure and I assure you, you will never pass or amount to anything.' As he said that I froze. He embarrassed me in front of my colleagues.

Words can be like poison. Immediately I got home after that event, I knew I had to fight a battle for my mind. I needed to expel all negative feelings to ensure that I would pass the exam. I had to overturn the surgeon's pronouncements. I began to flood my spirit with the positive things God has said about me. I opened the Scriptures and read the parts that promised me success. I confessed out loud, 'I will pass! I will pass!' In the end I did pass.

Pessimistic Comparisons

We usually fail to see our real selves and appreciate who we are. Quite easily, we get lost in the crowd! Some people disqualify themselves when approached to do certain things that they feel nervous about. They look at their insecurities and magnify them. 'Oh, I'm too short, too tall, too large, too thin, too old, too young, the list goes on.' I am so glad I finally got the sense that there was a great person hiding within me somewhere, who must come out.

You need to know that you are the best and the only *you* that God created.

Bad Incidents and Accidents

A feeling of being crippled can also come through having been abused or raped. These can leave one frigid and limited in all relationships. The act was the trauma, but the crippling results last longer. Other symptoms like promiscuity, rebelliousness or shyness stem from incidents in our lives where someone left us wounded. We act on the basis of our feelings because we have not forgiven ourselves for certain incidents that have happened to us at some stage in our lives.

A person may be sitting beside you in the congregation on a Sunday morning, dressed their best and proclaiming that they are a blessed, conquering overcoming child of the King. But inside they feel like a failure because of an image from their past. To them it is so vivid and real that it prevents them from conquering their today and strips them of a bright tomorrow.

MY STORY

As a teenager in the university, I got involved with drugs. I smoked 'dope' (cannabis) for two and a half years as this seemed like the 'hip' thing to do at the time. It was an age of teenage experimentation. This particular type of drug causes a loss of memory. One becomes absent-minded and paranoid. It also brings a detachment from reality so that, for the period that you are smoking it, you become emotionally and intellectually stunted. People who take drugs are often trying to escape reality. Reality is necessary to bring about maturity. When you face challenges in life and conquer them, they make you a stronger person. But if you try to escape them by blotting them out with drugs or alcohol or some other stimulant, you can never grow to become the person you were meant to be.

REALITY IS NECESSARY TO BRING ABOUT MATURITY.

Although I started off doing very well in school, my mind was affected quite badly by the use of the drugs. It also had an adverse effect on my language, my confidence and my speech. Because of my drug use, I started hanging around with the wrong type of crowd — people who used a lot of slang and 'broken English'. I discovered that for two and a half years I had been spaced out. I could no longer fully understand the medical books I was reading, and for the first time in my life I began to experience failure after failure. Where I had always enjoyed a long-term success as one of the top three students in my class, it was not long before I was called up for constantly being in the bottom third.

THE STAMMERING PROPHET

Towards the end of that time I became a committed Christian. I wondered at first whether my failures were due to my new faith. I refused to believe that the drugs had such a devastating effect on my abilities. I lacked self-confidence. Someone would say something to me and I would not be able to recall it after ten minutes. I was frustrated and began to stammer.

Here was I, called by God into His wonderful Kingdom with this new lease of life. God had begun to tell me that I would one day become a prophet and preach His Word. My first reaction was to laugh. I thought I misheard. 'Me, God? Don't You know that I am a stammerer?' I realised much later that we usually experience setbacks in the same areas that God intends to use us. Here I was with this destiny to speak for God but with no fluency or confidence, so that I thought that I could not speak clearly. The enemy of our souls knows what we are called to do, therefore his plan is to cripple us in our feet. God, evidently, has the last say! In spite of all the enemy tried in my life, I have been in the ministry of proclaiming God's transforming word for the last twelve years with signs following.

References:

Seamands, David. Putting Away Childish Thing. *Illinois, Victor Press, 1993.*

Chapter 5

THE PRINCE WITH
A BEGGAR'S MIND

Mephibosheth was a prince in the days just before King David began to reign. He was the son of Jonathan and grandson of King Saul. By virtue of his birth, he had the potential to become king at some point in his future. Both Jonathan and Saul died on the same day, when Mephibosheth was only five years old. At that age, he was still innocent and fragile. Unlike the members of royal families today, Mephibosheth had not yet been groomed to speak or carry himself in a princely manner. He had not undergone any special schooling or royal treatment. He did not know what it meant to be a child of a king.

When it became known that his father and grandfather had died in war, a nurse took Mephibosheth and fled with him in her arms in a bid to rush him to safety. While on the run, she accidentally dropped him (2 Samuel 4:4). He became crippled from this accident and was unable to walk again. Mephibosheth was taken to a far away wilderness called Lo Debar where he grew up as a poor beggar. Lo Debar was not only a slum, but was one of the worst places in which one could consider living at that time. It would be the equivalent of a member of the British royal family making his home and fending for himself in a downtown hostel for homeless boys!

A BEGGAR IN THE PALACE

Soon after David had been anointed king, he sought to honour the covenant he had made with Jonathan by showing kindness to anyone left of the descendants of Saul (1 Samuel 9:1-4). He learnt about Mephibosheth's existence and called for him. Upon hearing that the king had summoned him, Mephibosheth's first reaction was fear. He did not believe that his status was higher than that to which he had become accustomed. He referred to himself as a dead dog, suggesting that he did not see himself as worthy of being treated with much respect. Mephibosheth had difficulty receiving the king's honour because of an ingrained mindset of inferiority.

Today, people who have a poor self-image or low self-esteem, especially those who have experienced abuse, have trouble believing that they are worth much more than a dog. If a woman in that position is in a relationship with a man and he suddenly raises his hand, she will recoil instantly in fear, believing that he is about to hit her. She has become accustomed to men raising their hands to beat her.

Some men cannot approach a woman because of this same problem. They feel intimidated by the car she drives or the kind of clothes she wears. This hinders many men from getting married today. They see a woman to whom they are attracted but they have a 'Dead-Dog' mentality (i.e. they do not feel up to the woman's standard).

WHO GAVE YOU THAT NAME?

Why did Mephibosheth belittle himself in such a profound way? Firstly, the name was given to him long after his birth. His name had originally been Merib-Baal (1 Chronicles 8:34). People often get called nicknames and if you have not known them for long, you may not know what the real name is. Some people get so used to being called by their nicknames that they may even begin to introduce themselves by it.

Secondly, the name 'Mephibosheth' means 'living shame'. It literally means, 'This person is so shameful that he should really be dead!' Another translation suggests that it can be defined as 'scattering shame'. In other words, everywhere he goes he causes trouble and brings shame. He is clumsy and awkward.

A name can leave a stigma that follows you around for a long time. You may not bear a name that means 'living shame', but what people have called you may have characterised who you are. Because I was called 'lazy' all my life, it was difficult for me to break out of that image before people who knew me as 'the lazy one.' You do not have to be characterised by whatever you are called. You can change your environment, and prove to yourself that you are not what they called you.

IT WAS NOT YOUR FAULT

Just like Mephibosheth, who became crippled by accident, many of the crippling experiences in our lives are often caused by events beyond our control. Parents never ask for their children's permission before they start hitting each other in front of them. Some children have had to live through the trauma of watching their parents' marriage deteriorate until it finally ended in divorce.

Even after divorce or separation, the trauma continues. Insults are still exchanged between the parents — and from everyone else on both sides of the family — without any thought of sheltering the children from pain. These things affect the way one behaves as well as how one sees himself.

YOU ARE NOT WHAT YOU HAVE BEEN THROUGH

In the film *The Shawshank Redemption*, there is a particular scene that sticks in my mind because it was particularly unpleasant. A man who had been a prestigious accountant all his life suddenly found himself thrust into prison. He was in there for quite a number of years, but never forgot who he was. In order to escape from the prison, he had to swim through a sewage tank, full of human faeces. I know it sounds disgusting and unimaginable, but had he not gone through that terrible place, he would not have been able to achieve his freedom. It did not deter him because, in his mind, while he was going through the sewer, he constantly reminded himself of the destiny he saw ahead of him. He came through that nasty place, cleansed himself and moved on.

THOUGH THE ENEMY MAY REMIND US OF OUR PAST ON A REGULAR BASIS, WE KNOW WHO WE WERE BUT WE ALSO KNOW WHO WE HAVE BECOME

In the same way, we often need to go through a number of terrible or difficult times in our lives for a reason. If not, we may remain imprisoned in our past and do not attain the ultimate glory. Though the enemy may remind us of our past on a regular basis, we know who we were but we also know who we have become: a new creature, old things dispensed with and all things become new. God and His Word are always there to remind us that there is a place reserved for us and our future is bright.

Whether or not there is a place in your life that you do not want to remember, always know that there is a place for you in the Kingdom of God. When you come into your Father's house, you should know that it is your home, regardless of where you have come from, what you have lived through or where you have been. You have a place in the Palace.

Chapter 6

THE PLOT TO LIMIT &
DESTROY THE REAL YOU

From the day you were born, evil forces were deployed against you to hinder the full potential that God destined for your life. Events occur that are deliberately intended to stifle your vision, steal your destiny and destroy your confidence. These are strategic attacks instigated by the enemy of your soul.

SATAN'S STRATEGY

The enemy plans to destroy your potential with the same strategy he employed to oppress Israel and restrict their freedom. After the death of Joseph, a new Pharaoh was set over Egypt. The new king did not know how Joseph had saved Egypt from famine. All he saw was that his nation appeared to be overrun with Israelites. His response was a determination to oppress and eventually annihilate the Jews. He issued an edict to have the newborn Israelite baby boys killed on the 'birthing stool', and also laid additional burdens on the working adults.

The devil knew that there was a deliverer and prophet about to be born among the Hebrews, hence the decision to destroy God's children (many centuries later, he also stirred up Herod to kill all baby boys around the time of Jesus' birth). It turned out, however, that the more Pharaoh's taskmasters afflicted the Israelites, the more they flourished.

THREATENED BY OUR POTENTIAL

The children of Israel were not at that time enslaved to Egypt. They had been living in harmony with their neighbours without causing any harm or disturbance to anyone. Still, the new Pharaoh felt threatened by their potential. The enemy of our souls knows who we are as children of God. He is threatened by who we are in God. This is why he initiates affliction in the lives of believers. These afflictions should be an indication to us that we pose a potential threat to the enemy; they should also alert us to our latent abilities.

Whatever you believe to be the reason for your poor self-image or low self-esteem, the root cause is that the devil is afraid of your true potential. He knows well before you do that you are in a position to bring deliverance to people in some capacity. He is, therefore, desperate to prevent you from emerging into your destiny. His desire is to steal, kill and destroy (John 10:10) before you do the same to him!

SATAN SEEKS TO DESTROY OUR SELF-IMAGE

Unlike Pharaoh, Satan's antics are carried out with a little more stealth and subtlety. He *steals* by taking the Word of God out of our hearts and minds, and clouding our ability to recognise our significance in God. Doubt and fear robs us of the freedom to worship and commune with God, and the confidence that His love ensures. Satan *kills* by attacking our aspirations and dreams. He darkens the hope that we might one day exercise our gifts, achieve our ambitions, operate within our full potential and bring glory to God. Satan *destroys* by hindering the effect of our lives on the kingdom of God. He does this in envy and revenge that stems from having been ejected from his position and place in heaven.

When I counsel people who appear to have a poor self-image, I usually discover that they are called to do great things for God. They have a message to share, so much to give, and yet are shy and insecure. God created them for something far greater than they believe they can handle. Evidently, the devil launched his attack early enough to stop their great purpose from materialising.

Many marriages, for instance, are doomed from the start because one (or both) of the partners has no self-belief and often, he or she will have trouble believing in the other.

DEMONS FROM BIRTH

From the womb to the tomb, Satan diligently sets out to obscure our ability to grow spiritually, mentally and emotionally. As a result, He robs God of any glory we could have brought Him. He is systematic and strategic in his continuous bid to hi-jack our destiny. A preacher I know once had a vision. He saw that demons were assigned to babies as they were born in the hospital! The demons attached themselves to the spirit of each child to ensure their growth and morality is hampered in some way.

Perhaps you have wondered why this generation has produced so many unsavoury characters and a high degree of immorality compared to other generations, or the reason why there are more people on drugs, into violence, illicit relationships, scandalous and disgraceful living? One reason is the devil fears that a 'deliverer' is about to be birthed again. What is more, he knows that it is not just one deliverer, but a body of deliverers!

CATCH THEM YOUNG!

A whole spiritual nation is being prepared, made up of people who will soar in their gifts into lofty positions in the spiritual realm. They will take their place as a strong, mighty army against the rulers of darkness that have blinded God's people for far too long; an army, the like of which there has never been before. Satan is seeking to destroy this end-time generation because he fears its potential. He does not know exactly who would be doing what, but his strategy is to demoralise us mentally, emotionally and spiritually before we realise who we are.

MANY MARRIAGES, FOR INSTANCE, ARE DOOMED FROM THE START BECAUSE ONE (OR BOTH) OF THE PARTNERS HAS NO SELF-BELIEF AND OFTEN, HE OR SHE WILL HAVE TROUBLE BELIEVING IN THE OTHER.

GOD'S WISDOM

When the devil throws attacks at your life, God, in His wisdom, turns them around for your good. He uses the trauma you pass through as preparation for your destiny. The area of your disability, your apparent dysfunction, is more than likely the area into which God has called you to excel. Any area in your life where Satan has concentrated his attacks is the place of your strength. However, he will want you to believe that it is your weakness. Your most passionate frustration or Achilles' heel, with God's help, will be turned around to your field of deliverance. It will be the field in which your gift will soar and bring deliverance to others. This is the wisdom of God.

Kenneth Hagin, one of the foremost preachers of our time, an apostle of faith and an authority on divine healing, was converted from a very young age. For several years, he was so ill that he could not get out of bed. During that time, he had the opportunity to develop his faith. He decided to take God at His Word, and eventually, was propelled out of his sickbed. This triumph over his affliction was a demonstration of God's power and the basis for letting others know the working of God's power through the activation of the word of faith.

T.D. Jakes preaches emotional healing so powerfully today, because he endured a prolonged season as an emotional cripple. He was so distraught at the death of his father while a teenager, that for decades later he was still haunted by nightmares which left him with a sense of longing and loneliness. Although he was at this point both a husband and a father, inside he was still that little boy yearning for his absent father. One of the reasons his messages have so much power and anointing is that he sought healing from the Great Physician, in the Word of God. He has now become a voice of emotional healing in this generation.

THE AREA OF YOUR DISABILITY, YOUR APPARENT DYSFUNCTION, IS MORE THAN LIKELY THE AREA INTO WHICH GOD HAS CALLED YOU TO EXCEL.

WHAT IS THE MOUNTAIN IN YOUR WAY?

Between you and your destination lies an impediment, an intimidating inadequacy, a menacing mountain that must be removed. It is like an irritating little imp standing in your face and saying 'You can't go beyond this point. Who do you think you are? You can't talk, preach, sing, study, teach, sell, write... You better stop right where you are, you don't want to embarrass yourself, don't try it!' God knows who you are because He formed you to be that person. If you know you are called in a certain area, then stand on the Word of God, claim your promise and break through that impediment. Anything less is a lie.

I don't know what you are looking at, what imaginary inadequacies stare you in the face and taunt you with insinuations that you can never go beyond a certain point. Whatever it is, you have an alternative. You have the power to address it directly, head-on, and to overcome it. If you respond verbally and actually with the Word of God, your situation will begin to change.

GOD IS IN CONTROL

God is in control of your life. He is keeping watch over your destiny. Moses, the intended deliverer of Israel, was placed in a basket and left to float on the riverbank. It was the parent's only option to keep him from being killed by the Egyptian soldiers. The river was not a mild or placid stream, but a rushing alligator-infested stream into which other Hebrew babies had been thrown.

If God was not watching over Moses, he would certainly have lost his life.

Regardless of the atrocities that surround you, God has control over your life. You may go through adversities, but God will preserve you. That you presently have a negative self-image is not a permanent hindrance to your destiny. Moses was safe by the river because God ensured that somebody was strategically positioned to preserve him. God will change your situation around as you entrust yourself to Him.

God granted Moses divine protection, divine provision and divine favour. In the same way, the difficulties you face give the opportunity to fall into God's hands and receive His provision. When He is in control, your future is secure.

NO MATTER WHAT YOUR PAST, YOU CAN DETERMINE YOUR FUTURE.

Our upbringing did not mess us up. The fact that we may have been brought up in a dysfunctional atmosphere did not mess us up. The fact that we may have witnessed violence or abuse did not mess us up. Our parents' divorce (whether physical or emotional) did not mess us up. All of these experiences will have served as an opportunity for us to get into a deep and meaningful relationship with the One who knows the real meaning of love, and is able to turn our lives around for the better. We can then develop into a stronger, wiser generation and be used to deliver others into peace.

No matter what your past, you can determine your future. You are called. You are chosen, designed and equipped by God for a specific and critical role within His Kingdom. You need to grasp the truth of who you really are in spite of your afflictions, bad experiences and whatever you may have gone through in life. In this way, the devil is put to shame and God is glorified.

PART THREE

THE PRESCRIPTION

Chapter 7

NICE CLOTHES WON'T COVER YOUR INSECURITIES

When God made man, He gave him a job, a purpose and a beautiful wife. He also gave man everything that he needed for a pleasurable life. Adam wanted for nothing.

This scenario, however, did not last for ever. Both Adam and his wife Eve disobeyed God. The consequence of their action was death; not an immediate, physical death, but a gradual separation from God. Although they had been naked all the while, their sin brought fear, guilt, shame and insecurity. They had, originally, been clothed in the glory of God and were not preoccupied with themselves or self-conscious.

SIN LEADS TO DYSFUNCTION AND DEATH

One of the consequences of sin is separation from the life and presence of God. Adam once had regular conversations with God but he lost this fellowship through sin. If one were to sever a branch from a fruit tree, initially the leaves would remain green and the fruit luscious, but surely enough, both the fruit and leaves will begin to die. Amputating a limb from a human body would cause the limb to cease to function due to separation from its blood supply. In the same way, we were created to function within a certain environment, an environment surrounded by the presence of God. The moment we leave that environment and lose relationship with God, whether through sin, lack of prayer or backsliding, we are like a fish out of water and we begin to die spiritually.

When we operate outside of the environment or place where God has planted us, we no longer operate at our optimal level. Indications of a slow spiritual death or lack of communication with God can manifest themselves in a number of ways. These include a lack of peace or joy, feelings of inadequacy and incompleteness, the feeling of generally having to struggle in most areas of our lives.

Sin leaves us with feelings of guilt, shame and nakedness — like Adam and Eve, feeling naked and ashamed. It may not be apparent externally, but on the inside we feel that we ought to be walking with our heads bowed. Sin usually brings insecurity.

When we sin by being disobedient to the revealed will of God, by functioning outside His identity, calling and purpose for our lives, we are automatically operating in a dysfunctional manner. If we were to be operating within God's purpose for our lives, He would guide us all the way, open doors for us and confirm for us on a regular basis that we are in His will.

ADAM ONCE HAD REGULAR CONVERSATIONS WITH GOD BUT HE LOST THIS FELLOWSHIP THROUGH SIN.

Insecurity comes when someone is anxious because they are not well adjusted to life. It is a feeling of perpetual incompleteness. Every human being feels insecure at some point in life. It is similar to the feeling of having a poor self-image in that one is left with a vague feeling of inferiority, but insecurity is inherent in us even when we have not been scarred by some negative event that happened to us in our past.

I FEEL NAKED AND VULNERABLE

The symptoms of insecurity include a feeling of always wanting to cover oneself with something. After Adam and Eve realised that they were naked (Genesis 3:7), they dressed themselves in leaves in a futile attempt to conceal their vulnerability. They could no longer stand before God with a clear conscience. They were embarrassed by their nakedness.

In the same way, anyone with a low self-esteem, whatever the cause, will have the constant need to cover up his insecurities before people. Clothes, cars and cottages are presented as a front to hide the real condition of the heart. This is man's way of dealing with a damaged life. The question is, how long can it last?

INSECURITY COMES WHEN SOMEONE IS ANXIOUS BECAUSE THEY ARE NOT WELL ADJUSTED TO LIFE. IT IS A FEELING OF PERPETUAL INCOMPLETENESS.

God sees through these antics and knows the state of our lives. 'Fig-leaves' do not hinder His vision. Even the night is as clear as day before Him. The irony is that no matter how much we dress up or cover up, we are never truly satisfied with ourselves. Undergoing plastic surgery when there is hardly anything noticeably 'wrong' is an example of the vanity that stems from a low self-image. Anorexia Nervosa and Bulimia are both dire indications of the same problem. Evidently, man cannot help himself but needs the intervention of God. One would have thought the likes of Lady Diana, Michael Jackson and Elvis Presley would be the happiest people ever. But with all the wealth, power and privileges they had, they still felt dissatisfied with who they were.

Another kind of cover-up illustrating a possible insecurity issue is the tendency to look for someone else to blame — the feeling that other people are the problem. When God asked Adam what he had done, he blamed his sin on his wife. *'The woman who you gave me...'* He was passing the buck to avoid being judged. No-one wants to be perceived as being incomplete or having a fault. We would rather point our finger at someone else as the cause than admit our condition and receive healing. If only we knew that God requires nothing more than a honest confession of our true condition! Repentance and confession is a key to inner healing.

WHY AM I AFRAID TO REVEAL MY TRUE SELF?

A certain psychologist, John Powell, posed the question 'Why are we afraid to tell people who we really are?' He had come to realise that we all have a real self, i.e. our inner self, which often appears to be at odds with the world around us. Outside our true self we feel there is some negative external factor telling us that we are not good enough or that we are the 'odd one out'.

Because we sometimes believe that negative factor suggesting that our true self is somehow lacking, we slip on a phoney exterior to disguise our true selves. This results in scenarios where we are desperately unhappy on the inside but wear a bright smile on the outside to avoid probing questions. Or we flatter people whom we don't really like, to avoid any potential confrontation that might unmask our true feelings. People change their voices and dress in clothes in which they may not feel comfortable, in order to 'fit in' and be accepted.

WHY ARE WE AFRAID TO REVEAL
WHO WE REALLY ARE?

John Powell says: because we are afraid that if we reveal who we really are, 'You might not like who you see, and that's all I have.'

Why are we afraid to show people who we really are? Perhaps the answer might be that we are afraid of having our real selves rejected. We go to great lengths to protect ourselves from suffering the pain of rejection. If I show you who I really am, you may run away from me and leave me feeling naked. With nothing left to hide behind, where does that leave me?

GOD WILL NOT REJECT YOU

When God calls your name, He has no intention of rejecting you. He knows everything about you including your inadequacies. Perhaps you are embarrassed because of your nakedness. God is not. Adam did not need to hide or blame Eve. Repentance would have led to restoration.

In spite of your weaknesses, there is still a great destiny ahead of you. Feelings of inadequacy and a lack of confident should not deter you from responding to God. The last thing you want to do is cover up and pretend before God.

Jeremiah felt inadequate when God approached him; he felt like a mere child. 'I do not know how to speak; I am only a child' (Jeremiah 1:6). Moses too, immediately pointed out his speech impediment, insisting that he was not fit for the job of delivering the Jews because he was '...slow of speech and of tongue' (Exodus 4:10). When God met with Gideon, He addressed him as a 'mighty man of valour!', and told him to save Israel from the hand of the Midianites. Gideon responded immediately by declaring the image he had of himself — basically saying that he was the lowliest member of a really poor family, from a low clan, the least in his father's house (Judges 6:12-14). As if God would not know who he was! If God calls you a mighty man, that is who you are. Start seeing yourself that way.

Notice that none of these people ever said 'Oh yes, Lord, I can do it! I have the credentials, the ability, the confidence, the strength, the qualifications... I am well able, Lord. Glad you picked me. Good choice!' No. Each one of them felt afraid and inadequate. Notwithstanding, God used them to accomplish great things.

You can tell God the true state of your heart because He is the source of your transformation. Do not cover up the obvious. Report your situation to Him and He will transport you to the other side of your purpose in life. He is able to heal every wound and issue in your life as you make a decision to expose them to Him.

References:

Powell, John. Why Am I Afraid To Tell You Who I Am? *Illinois, Argus Communications, 1969.*

Chapter 8

EXPOSED FOR HEALING

Y ou do not have to be a rocket scientist to know that our society is very sick. You only need to watch the news, the various talk shows or read the news-papers to know that people's ailments in today's world are becoming more complex than ever before. We see and hear incidents of little children being abducted by paedophiles who rape and kill them in order to cover the evidence. Little kids take guns to school to kill their school mates and teachers. People openly confess, without remorse or embarrassment, that they had affairs with their best friend's girlfriend, sister's husband etc. We hear of fathers who consistently rape their own daughters.

How did we become like this? Most of the above listed issues have their root in spiritual, psychological and emotional problems most of which started in the childhood of the villains. The villains themselves were one time victims, and because their pain was repressed for years without any hope of respite or palliation it manifested itself as hatred, perversion or other antisocial behaviour.

Society is hurting and in need of real healing, but in spite of the advancement in technology, recombinant DNA technology and space travels, we have not been able to find the cure for our social diseases.

Psychology, psychotherapy, psychiatry and aromatherapy only present temporary palliation and little in the form of relief for what is a very real and growing problem. What we need is a real solution to a very deep problem.

THE ROOT OF OUR EVIL

At the heart of the problem is the issue of abandonment and rejection, which has its roots in the rejection and abandonment of God and His ways. As discussed in the last chapter, when we lose our connection with our Maker (our source), the effect can be disastrous.

The pain and complexities we suffer in our communities are the result of our breaking away from God and breaking His statutes and ordinances for our lives. Hence we have become a broken and fragmented society. One of the major recognisable causes of antisocial behaviour today is the fragmentation of the family, where over half of every marriage ends up in divorce. With over 60% of children raised in single parent homes, this has indeed had a negative effect on our society. Some one said, 'If we fail to build better homes we will have to build more prisons.'

What does this have to do with the issues you struggle with emotionally or psychologically? If we do not get the healing we require in our soul, we may just become further statistics of society's misfits and diseases.

THE MAIN PROBLEM

The major problem with this society is not the AIDS virus or cancer, but a lack of love and a neglect of God and His values. Also, most of the problems outlined above are the result of selfish, ignorant, rebellious parents who abuse their position, abdicate their responsibility, abandon their children or are amateur in their parenting methods. These problems can either be traced directly or indirectly to the absence of a father's love or parental care in the raising up of children. You will find that the issues that we struggle with today have their roots in rejection by an authority figure, or by someone who ought to have been there to love, esteem, protect, validate, nurture and care for us.

'IF WE FAIL TO BUILD BETTER HOMES WE WILL HAVE TO BUILD MORE PRISONS'.

I believe that our true healing will come first from confronting and dealing with our covered-up issues and also from addressing the root cause of our ailments by understanding how we can compensate for our losses.

The first step towards healing the wounds of our past will be to confront the problem.

DO NOT DENY THE PAIN

In my days as a practising doctor, we were taught something about testing and examining patients. If they suddenly cried out when certain areas of their body is touched, it was important not to ignore the response. We were expected to go back to that area and press it again and fully examine it. This is necessary not because doctors like to cause people pain or hear their patients crying out, but because there could be an abnormality in that place or something else that is causing trouble. It is only wise to treat it if you know exactly what to do and how to do it, otherwise you will make matters worse.

We must allow God to heal us of our secret wounds; if not, it will cause us serious pain throughout the rest of our lives. And like many physical wounds, it may result in dysfunction or disability.

I BELIEVE THAT OUR TRUE HEALING WILL COME FIRST BY CONFRONTING AND DEALING WITH OUR COVERED-UP ISSUES.

In the same way, when there is an issue in a relationship that frequently flares up and causes arguments, a wise person will recognise that behind the outburst there is something causing pain. It is better not to address the issue immediately while the person is raging, but to wait until a calmer, safer moment to try to deal with the problem behind the pain. It is a known fact that dogs that have an injured limb often bark, snap and even bite anyone who goes near them (including their owners) in a bid to protect themselves from suffering any further harm. God has been trying to heal you of your past wounds or pain, but His attempts at healing you may seem as if He is causing you more pain.

When performing an operation to remove a foreign body or whatever is causing inflammation, the doctor will delve a little deeper and remove the debris and pus surrounding the site. If this is not done, the area will become septic and eventually lead to amputation or even death. When dealing with these deep personal wounds or issues, it will cause some pain. But the probing is necessary to remove the foreign body in order for our wounds to be thoroughly healed.

Hence we need to be honest with ourselves, agree that we really do have a problem and name it for what it is, before we can truly find healing.

Many of us would rather live with our sores than confront the issues that have led to our emotional pains. Although the healing process is quite painful, it could lead to a place of comfort and wholeness. Healing is a process that requires great patience and persistence.

HAS YOUR WOUND BEEN INFECTED?

Time alone will not heal a wound. Like physical wounds, an emotional wound, if left unattended or undressed, will become infected.

In natural medicine, for a wound to heal properly, it has to be cleared of debris or dead tissue and cleaned with a disinfectant. This is called debridment. This is because wounds attract infective organisms, which fester or thrive on the wound and produce lethal toxins that can be fatal.

Emotional and psychological wounds also attract infective organisms that can have fatal consequences. Demonic spirits are attracted to deep emotional wounds. For instance, where there has been very deep rejection by one parent or both, there will be a vulnerability to being infected by spirits of low self-esteem, fear, and in some cases, perversion and homosexuality. Cases of very intense physical, sexual or verbal abuse by parents will attract a spirit of rebellion, witchcraft or self-destruction and even suicidal tendencies. These spirits are usually the ones responsible for the extreme anti-social behaviour we see in our society today. They take advantage of people's wounds and pain and demonise them to the extent that they begin to behave abnormally.

WHO WILL RELIEVE ME OF MY PAIN?

We need the intervention of the Great Physician, the one who is able to heal the battered and comfort the shattered. God's soothing touch and healing balm are able to penetrate where no surgeon's knife can reach, where no physician's prescription can permeate, and no psychiatrist's counsel can address. God can and will heal our deepest wounds, be it our deep insecurities, low self-worth, poor self-image feelings of rejection and abandonment, if we let Him.

He says in Jeremiah 8:11,

'They dress the wound of my people as though it were not serious. "Peace, peace," they say, when there is no peace.'

God is interested and committed to your recovery from the past hurts that have plagued you for years. He wants to take away the excruciating pain you feel in your heart and heal your deepest wounds. After wounds are probed and cleaned out they are bandaged up and the patient is given analgesics to relieve the pain. He says, 'Come to me all you who labour and are heavy laden and I will give you rest.' Speak to Him and the shepherd of your soul will bring healing and relief to your aching soul. He knows where you are hurting and He knows how to heal you.

DEMONIC SPIRITS ARE ATTRACTED TO DEEP EMOTIONAL WOUNDS.

LEARNING TO WALK AGAIN

After we have confronted the fact that we have an issue, dealt with the root cause, removed any lethal foreign body and relieved the pain, the next thing doctors tend to do is hand the patient over to a physiotherapist. Their job is to help to retrain the patient to use the limb or part of the body that had been rendered useless or immobile because of the trauma and the healing process.

GOD WILL BEGIN TO PROVOKE US TO LOVE AGAIN AFTER A REJECTION, TRUST AGAIN AFTER A BETRAYAL

Similarly, with the healing of an emotional trauma, God will move us and bring us to a place where we begin to challenge our immobility or our stagnation in life caused by past traumatic incidents. He begins to train us to do the things that we thought we could not do by reason of the incident or the accident we had experienced earlier in life, things which had incapacitated us in our emotions.

God will begin to provoke us to love again after a rejection, trust again after a betrayal, to come out of our comfort zone, to have faith again and venture out after a failure. He challenges us to rise up and walk even though we may again stumble and fall, so that we will eventually stand on our own two feet, not needing crutches, without any dependence on anyone to comfort us, hold us up, be there for us or to stand by us. We would come to a point where we will not only be standing on our own two feet but will also be strong enough to pull other people out of their own dilemma. Have you been in a certain condition for a long time? Jesus is saying to you today, 'Do you want to be made well?' The choice is yours. 'Rise up, and walk...' The Lord will strengthen you as you trust Him to bring you to a place of complete and total healing.

References:

Stringer, Doug. The Fatherless Generation (Hope For A Generation in Search of Identity), *Shippensburg, Destiny Image, 1995.*

Chapter 9

WHO WILL TELL ME WHO I REALLY AM?

The quest for identity resides in every human being because God placed it in us. He alone knows the answer to the question: 'Who am I?' He put in us this unanswered question so that we can return to Him for the unique answer.

God, in His wisdom, set up the family system to ensure that every child receives the definition of his or her identity and the necessary nurturing that will secure its manifestation. Unfortunately, the family system has almost become non-existent and has become a breeding ground for insecurity and social dysfunction.

ALL IS NOT LOST

Where the family has failed, God makes up the difference. God set up the family unit to model, pattern or foreshadow the type of relationship God has with us, and it is from Him that every family derives its identity.

'...The father, from whom his whole family in heaven and earth derives its name' (Ephesians 3:14,15)

The family was originally designed to prefigure and demonstrate God's love and was intended to nurture us into becoming who we were created to be. But where our family experience is less than ideal or totally non-existent. All is not lost for God, through His son Jesus, has accepted us into the Beloved and given us a model to follow.

WHO WAS JESUS' FATHER?

The paternity of Jesus is an issue that has always been in question from the time of His birth until now. The Scriptures declare that Mary conceived Jesus as she was overshadowed by the Holy Spirit.

'How will this be... since I am a virgin?'... 'The Holy Spirit will come upon you, and the power of the Most High will over-shadow you.' (Luke 1:34,35)

Hence God was the 'biological' father and Joseph was the 'surrogate' father. This is important to note because while Jesus was being raised there was the issue in the community about Him being born an illegitimate child. He was raised under dark suggestions of neighbours, and had to live under rumours and gossip about the mysterious circumstances around His birth. But in spite of all this, His most natural inclination in an attempt to quell the rumours would have been to claim Joseph as His natural father. But he chose to claim his 'Heavenly Father'. There is an important lesson or model to note. He did this because we receive our 'Name' or identity from our fathers. Children are identified by their father's surname. The sense of who we are comes essentially from our father.

This is the reason why it was clearly stated and documented just before the genealogy of Jesus Christ in Luke 3:22-23 after his baptism that

'A voice came from heaven: "You are My Son, whom I love; with you I am well pleased."'

The genealogy now proceeded to say;

'Now Jesus himself was about thirty years old when he began his ministry. He was the son, so it was thought, of Joseph...'

It was clearly stated and re-emphasised in scripture that Joseph was only the assumed natural father. Why is this important? And why did they further list the genealogy of Jesus up to both the son of Adam the Son of God?

'The son of Seth, the son of Adam, the Son of God'. (Luke 3:38).

LIKE FATHER LIKE SON

Jesus' genealogy was listed and traced back to Adam from his real father (God) and his 'surrogate' father Joseph (as was supposed), because the writer was trying to show that Jesus' lineage was not from Joseph who was a descendant of fallen Adam, but He was directly of the genealogy of our Father in heaven. This is important because sons receive the resemblance in nature, likeness and genetic make-up from their fathers. We receive both good and bad traits from whichever father gave us birth.

JESUS DID NOT COME FROM ADAM

'This is the written account of Adam's line. When God created man, he made him in the likeness of God... When Adam had lived 130 years, he had a son in his own likeness, in his own image; and he named him Seth.' (Genesis 5:1&3)

According to the above scripture God created man originally in His own likeness (i.e. we were just like Him in nature) 'A chip off the old block,' as the saying goes. Until Adam sinned and gave birth to Seth who was born in the likeness of Adam, whose nature had become sinful and personality had become insecure, his self-worth was in question and his image of himself had become distorted. This is the root of our poor self-image, because we receive our identity from less than perfect parents.

WHO NAMED YOU?

To make matters worse it is stated that Adam went on to name his son 'Seth' which means that Adam took on the responsibility of calling his son whatever he wanted. He gave him his identity. Many people are suffering untold pain today because of the name or the thing they have been called. To name means to label. It is a means of identifying a person. We have been called all sort of ugly names by people in authority over us and those names have stuck to us. Imagine: Jacob's name means 'Deceiver' and Jabez's mother named him 'Sorrow'. What did you grow up being called?

THE BENEFITS OF HAVING GOD AS YOUR FATHER

Jesus called and prayed to His heavenly father many times. It is obvious He was more aware of His father in heaven than the one on earth because there is a great benefit He was trying to model for us in this relationship with His heavenly father. These benefits include:

Regeneration

When we received Jesus into our heart, regeneration occurred within us. This means a changing of our genes, i.e. our paternity became a divine one, and indeed we became 'born again', born of the Spirit and seed of God. (In computer language it will be said that our microchip was upgraded or our hard disk changed all together!).

With the recognition and awareness of having God as your father you can now walk in the fullness of the benefits of your relationship with Him and receive what was absent in your natural relationship with your parents.

If our relationship with our earthly parent is or was less than ideal, we can receive what we missed out on emotionally, psychologically and spiritually from our heavenly father. God is able to make it up to you as you learn to 'Rise up and walk' closely with Him. We can receive the same benefits Jesus enjoyed from having God as His father. You can develop a real and intimate relationship with our heavenly father just as Jesus did.

Identity

As mentioned earlier, the genealogy of Jesus states that He came directly from the father; hence He received His sense of identity from God and not Joseph. Even though He was raised in Joseph's house He did not adopt Joseph's image or attributes. He developed Himself in the image and likeness of God the father. He understood that He was holy just as His father in heaven is holy (1 Peter 1:16). He did not grow up having any of the hang-ups of Joseph's earthly ancestors. God's original intent for us is stated in the scripture below.

> **'They know nothing, they understand nothing. They walk about in darkness... I said, "You are 'gods'; you are all sons of the Most High," But you will die like mere men; you will fall like every other ruler.' (Psalm 82:5,6).**

When we receive our identity from God the father we can live supernatural lives and walk in the same mental class as, and with similar attributes to God (e.g. love, holiness, mercy). It is only when you have the image of God that you can have dominion in the affairs of this life.

'Then God said, "Let us make man in our image, in our likeness, and let them have rule.' (Genesis 1:26)

In the Hebrew tradition it was the father's responsibility to raise the son and tell him who he was and what he would become in life.

Name

Like Jesus we can also receive a new name from our heavenly father. Jesus was given His name by God through the angel Gabriel: 'You will be with child and give birth to a son, and you are to give him the name Jesus' (Luke 1:31). His name was not left at the mercy of His earthly parents, because He had a special mission to fulfil and names go a long way in determining whom or what we become.

Whatever you were named from birth or in the course of your life could go a long way towards hindering or enhancing your destiny. Jabez was called 'Sorrow' because he was born in sorrow. He ended up causing much sorrow in life, until he prayed and God changed his lot in life. When God decided to bless Abram, He changed his name to Abraham (meaning 'Father of many nations'). He changed Jacob's name (meaning deceiver) to Israel (meaning 'Prince of God'). Regardless of what you have been called, God can give you a new name.

Purpose

Jesus' relationship with his father birthed in Him a sense of purpose and passion for His father's business, even as early as the age of 12 years.

'Wist ye not that I must be about my father's business?' (Luke 2:49 KJV).

Even though He had known His natural father and worked with him in the carpenter's business, He was still passionate about pursuing the assignment that God had sent Him to fulfil. A father's trade can have a great determining effect on the profession one chooses in life. I remember wanting to become an architect like my dad as early as 7 years of age.

Affirmation

Everyone looks to their father to tell them who they are. We look to our parents for affirmation or validation when we do things. We would love our parents to watch us while we perform in the school play, we would want them to attend our graduation ceremony and say well done, but if not we can still receive God's own endorsement like Jesus did after his baptism.

'And a voice came from heaven: "You are my Son, whom I love; with you I am well pleased."' (Luke 3:22)

Did you notice that this was said before Jesus even commenced His earthly ministry? This is a major antidote against the pressure to perform. Regardless of what we do or don't do, God is already pleased with us before we commence our assignment in life. The devil tried to get Jesus to do a number of things, but Jesus was not interested in proving His sonship, since He already knew and had been told by the Father, He was the Son of God.

Security

Fear is a lack of trust and lies at the root of insecurity in life. Many people suffer from major insecurities in their adult life because of the unfavourable, hostile and non-trusting environment in which they were nurtured while growing up. It is said that when a little infant's basic needs are not met or are unattended to while she is crying for her parents' attention, that baby will grow up feeling insecure and thinking that the world is a harsh place to live in.

Jesus was secure in who He was and He had an abundant, positive expectation of life. We see that at His temptation in the wilderness even the devil was aware of the fact that God would send His angels to protect Him if anything tried to hurt Him (Luke 4:10-11). You can feel secure in the fact that God knows your future and He knows your future is bright and secure. As the scripture says, 'Perfect love casts out fear (insecurity)' (1 John 4:18).

Love

Like Jesus you can also enjoy and know the unchangeable unconditional love of God the father. God loves His children not because of what we can do for Him but in spite of what we have done. Even our parents' love can be conditional, but we can rest in the fact that God loves us regardless.

Some may want to take His love and mercy for granted, but as God is merciful He is also just. He is a good father and good parents lovingly correct their children. God loves you too much to leave you the way you are.

PART FOUR

THE PROGNOSIS

Chapter 10

EQUIPPED FOR A PURPOSE

If you were to ask God the purpose for which He created you, the answer would be, 'For a position far superior to your current function and greater than you could imagine.' God knows why you are here. He can, and will, help you to achieve your calling and true potential when you ask Him.

Helen Keller was destined to be a leader in her generation but she was born deaf, dumb and blind. She came to discover who she really was and she was not deterred by what she could have become. Her spirit, drive and determination propelled her into greatness and she is still a beacon today even in her death.

CREATED FOR A UNIQUE PURPOSE

When we seek employment, we look for a position we think we can fill. If we have had experience in a certain field, we might look for something with a similar title, or a job description that matches what we believe we can do. We go for the interview, we get the job and we are usually given a title for our position. For example, we might be introduced to our new colleagues as the 'Senior Financial Advisor' the 'Marketing Consultant' or 'the Dean', and so on.

In the same way, we have received an identity from our Creator for a position on His earth. The remedy against competition and rivalry is, to be assured that we all have a distinct position given to us by God for which there is no equal. Before we were born He 'ordained us and sanctified us' (see Jeremiah 1:5). We need to understand God's assignment to us as individuals. When we know the specific vocation into which we have been called, we will not feel the need to contend with anyone for a particular position.

A pastor who has been called to oversee a church of two hundred people need not feel less significant than the pastor of a congregation of two thousand. It is not the quantity that counts. As long as he is genuinely serving the Lord with the flock that God has placed in his care, he has no reason to be envious. If he spends all his time and energy trying to drum up more members, he may miss the message God is trying to share through him. The same goes for a Senior Executive who has a hundred employees under his charge. If he tries to act like a CEO of a multinational corporation with a thousand employees he is bound to become frustrated.

GOD KNOWS YOUR SEASON

If we understand God's assignment for our own lives, and we focus on that as the benchmark against which we measure our progress and success, we are on the right track and need not envy anyone else. We may think the grass is greener on the other side, but fail to recognise that the grass on the other side also has to be mowed and cared for in order to remain so attractive. When we see someone who has achieved something for which we have been striving, we need not feel despondent. We need to ascertain whether we are ordained to pursue the kind of success they have achieved. If we do not do so, achieving the same things would probably not benefit us because it would be outside the will of God for our lives.

WHATEVER WE SAY ABOUT OURSELVES, WE WILL EVENTUALLY BECOME.

WAIT FOR YOUR SEASON

We also need to determine whether it is the right time or season for things to happen in our lives. Just because something has happened in the life of someone else does not mean it is time for it to happen in yours. When we try to invoke some event in our lives before we are ready to handle it or are prepared for the response or consequences, we could end up in a worse state than if we had left it alone.

Only God knows when our season is, and when we feel taunted by another person's early success we need to firstly be happy for them and rejoice with them. We should also stand in confidence and thank God that He, as our Creator, is working out great things to bless us in our own lives within His perfect timing. We just need to trust Him and be patient.

WATCH WHAT YOU SAY ABOUT YOURSELF

It is important for us to appreciate that our words, particularly those spoken about ourselves, have a profound effect upon us. Whatever we say about ourselves, we will eventually become. The Bible says that whatever a man ponders within his heart he will declare with his mouth. We can, therefore, determine what a person thinks of himself by what we hear him *say* about himself.

When I first understood from God that I was called to be a preacher, I had apprehensions in much the same way as Jeremiah did. I looked around at the other pastors I knew and was suddenly preoccupied with their height compared to my mine! I figured that in order to be a great pastor one must have presence, and in order to have presence one must be tall. It may sound ludicrous now, but at the time it was a real fear. I could not overcome the fact that other pastors were taller than I was, and therefore they must be able to pastor more effectively! I asked God time and time again why on earth He was sending me, knowing that I was not as tall as the other pastors. The only answer that constantly came back from God was '*Before*' (Jeremiah 1:4-10).

BEFORE YOU WERE BORN

It comforted me to hear God remind me that 'before' He formed me in my mother's womb, He knew what He had called me to do. Long *before*. Before I could speak, before I could read, before I was ever to pick up a Bible, God had me in mind way ahead of time and God knows exactly what He is doing. I was to hold on to this truth again and again in the early days of my ministry. I came to realise that I have the components and the capacity, I am configured to perform His work and to preach what He has called me to preach. It gradually helped to allay my fears, and the foolish notion that my stature could somehow affect His ability to speak through me or to use me as His vessel on this earth.

The main point is to remember that God is our Maker, our source and our ability. When we function within His realm, there is nothing to be insecure about. Jeremiah was overly concerned with other people's reactions towards him, but God had to remind him, just as He gently reminds us, not to look at other people's responses but to depend on Him alone.

YOU ARE GIFTED

God has placed a gift within each one of us, which He is able to use for His glory. No matter how little confidence we have, how little we think of ourselves, regardless of our doubts, our fears, our low self-esteem or poor self-image, we each have a gift that in the right setting will cause us to shine and bring glory to our Maker. We need to get to a place where we understand and appreciate our gift and are using it to its full potential. Our gift will put us over and above every situation and circumstance and move us from obscurity into the limelight (Proverbs 18:16). This is something that God has placed within us, that when used appropriately, will bring us security and remove all of our insecurities. (To find out more about your hidden abilities, read my earlier book *Discover Your Hidden Treasures*).

You may or may not think much of yourself right now, but when you discover what you are here to do you will value your life, your calling and your destiny. Look at it this way. If you knew you were expecting a letter from the Queen with a very large cheque inside it, the postman would suddenly become very important to you. The same postman, whom you barely acknowledge in the mornings on your way to work, would rapidly become your most important visitor. You would pace up and down your street looking for him, half an hour earlier than he would normally arrive. The envelope would become very important to you. The envelope that is worth just a few pennies would catch your eye and you would tear it open with anticipation. The cheque inside is what makes both the envelope and the postman more valuable to you than you would ever have considered them to be. If the postman decided not to come that day, you would not receive your cheque.

GIFT BEARERS ARE INVALUABLE

What I am illustrating is that the message makes the carrier of the message important. The gift makes the bearer of the gift important. Whatever it is you are called to do makes you an important person, regardless of the way you feel about yourself. God sent you on an assignment, and that is what makes you important. You need to carry your gift with respect and dignity, which is why you must carry yourself in the same way. When you begin to operate in the area and the strength of your gifting, you automatically become more attractive and appealing.

EQUIPPED FOR MY PURPOSE

My brother had a friend who also happened to be a backing singer for a famous female star in the world of popular music. Everywhere she went she was asked to sing and she sang really well. I remember one episode when, having recently become a Christian, I was in a car with both of them and a couple of their friends. I happened to be in a really peaceful mood. I started singing quietly to myself and praising God, using a worship song that was in my heart at the time. All of a sudden my brother and his friends began laughing at me and told me to stop singing because they thought I had such an awful voice. His friend the backing singer had not ventured her opinion. He asked her if she thought my voice was really that bad. She paused for thought and said, 'Do you know you have a magnificent radio presenter's voice?' I was so moved. She could have agreed with the others but chose a more diplomatic path. She looked for something good to say about my voice and turned the whole situation around.

It turned out ten years later that I did start broadcasting my own radio programme, and the very first thing the producer said was 'You have an excellent radio voice'!

I heard of a vicar who was conducting the funeral of a man who had not lived what one would call an exemplary life. Now, vicars are under a lot of pressure in these sorts of situations to say something good about the dear departed — only in this case the man had been such a rogue that it was almost impossible to meet the challenge! After a long while, the vicar looked around the congregation and back into the coffin and finally found to his relief that he was able to say: 'He had nice teeth!'.

LOOK UP FROM WHERE YOU ARE, THERE IS GREATNESS AWAITING YOU!

Perhaps that is a lesson to us all. Whenever we are asked to give our opinion to someone, particularly someone who already has a poor self-image, the best thing to do would be to find something good to say that would turn the situation around for good.

DON'T LET YOUR HANDICAP STOP YOU

If you have ever felt inadequate about anything in this life, any insecurity or apprehension, and you wonder how on earth God could consider using you for a particular job, just know that He knows you are the right candidate for that position.

Jeremiah had been ordained as a prophet to nations from before he was in his mother's womb (Jeremiah 1:4-9). As we know, Jeremiah instantly suggested that God should look for someone with a more adequate résumé, and believed himself to be the wrong choice for the position. When I first began a television ministry, we mainly had guest speakers. My initial role was to introduce them, turn over the program to the speaker and round up the programme at the end of the session. Although I was only on camera for a few moments, it took a number of takes before I finally got it right. I had not yet developed enough confidence for television work, not having been familiar with the medium. I think I can safely say that, at that time, I knew a little of what Jeremiah was going through.

PIANOS WERE MADE TO PLAY MUSIC

There are things that you know you ought to do, but you have told yourself that you are unable to do them. You have those limitations in your mind even though there are stirrings in your spirit. The limitations are just imaginary because there is nothing God cannot do. It would be like a piano telling its maker that it could not play music because it is too small and has been used by terrible players in the past so the music comes out badly. The piano was made to bring joy to many. There is nothing your Maker does not know about you that cannot be overcome in order that you achieve your full potential.

It is time for you to embrace your purpose in life irrespective of any handicap. Do not let your past dictate your future. The value you add to other people's lives is more important than wallowing in self-pity and depression. Look up from where you are, there is greatness awaiting you!

References:

Fola-Alade, Sola. Discover Your Hidden Treasure, *London, Vision Media Communications, 2002.*

Chapter 11

THE FUTURE IS IN YOUR HANDS

(Raising Extraordinary Children)

In our parents' generation, a lot of people had no clue as to how to raise ordinary children, let alone extraordinary children. This left parents in the subsequent generation with an even greater challenge. First, there is the challenge of raising children in such a way that they avoid becoming dysfunctional. Secondly, parents have a challenge to rise above the norm in parenting skills so that their children can excel in as many ways possible.

In order to raise children who come from ordinary homes but who have extraordinary minds, the home must first of all be stable and secure. The stable home is the nurturing ground for great minds of future generations.

Jonathan Edwards was a preacher in the first half of the eighteenth century whose sermons stirred the revival called 'The Great Awakening'. He and his wife Sarah had eleven children who all turned out exceptional. Their descendants were traced and were all found to have excelled in their respective generations. Among their grandchildren and great grandchildren numbered college presidents, professors, over a hundred lawyers and a law school dean. There were also physicians and a dean of a medical school. On the legal side, the Edwardses' descendants included judges, senators, mayors, state governors and a United States Vice President.

Jonathan and Sarah Edwards were able to raise phenomenal offspring from relatively humble beginnings. The climate of a stable home and a stable marriage nurtures great children. The Bible gives us a recipe for a stable home.

AN ATMOSPHERE OF AGREEMENT

In Matthew 18:19, the power of agreement is mentioned: 'Again, I tell you that if two of you on earth agree about anything you ask for it will be done for you by my Father in heaven.' Most parents' dream is that their children will succeed and leave a mark in the sands of time. God, in His infinite wisdom and mercy has given the platform of marriage, upon which two parents can stand and agree on any issue. Once the parents stand together in agreement in prayer, according to God's divine will regarding the future of their children, He has promised to honour their requests.

To establish His promise even further, God goes on to promise: 'For where two or three come together in my name, there I am with them' (Matthew 18:20). It is astonishing that a third person is added here, as we can strengthen our prayer by encouraging the child to be the third person standing in agreement. In other words, God has said He will respond to two parents who agree in prayer, but if at all possible, where a child acts as the third person agreeing regarding his or her own extraordinary destiny, He is in their midst. God's presence will help to nurture and raise the children.

THE RIGHT ENVIRONMENT

The enemy knows exactly what the recipe for a successful family is and will try at every opportunity to destroy any agreement formed. Almost immediately after the parents stand in agreement in prayer concerning their children, Satan will try to challenge the parents' faith.

THE CLIMATE OF A STABLE HOME AND A STABLE MARRIAGE NURTURES GREAT CHILDREN.

My younger son recently developed a life-threatening disease. My wife and I were naturally concerned and we prayed intensely over our boy. During prayer, it was revealed to me that this child was evidently destined for great things, which therefore posed a threat to Satan's kingdom. If you want to know what is important to God, take a look at what the devil diligently attacks.

THE ATTACK ON MARRIAGES

Often, in loving homes, the enemy will employ tactics to try to split parents apart, cause discord and even introduce the subject of divorce into an otherwise harmonious environment. His strategy is to distract couples from creating an atmosphere where children can blossom into strong, centred individuals who will one day glorify God. Once Satan succeeds in provoking friction in the home, he knows he has hindered the parents' desire to pray and agree together, and therefore damages the possibility of an extraordinary child being raised.

ABSENT PARENTS OPEN THE BACK DOOR

Satan will do all he can to fragment the home. This may manifest for example in the husband being away a lot of the time. An absent, adulterous, abdicating, abusing or alcoholic parent who is rarely home is not in a position to stand in agreement in prayer with the family and prevent the arena being created where God can be welcomed into their midst. The adverse effects of a spiritually unstable home on children are virtually the same as if the children come from a broken home. This can also be the entry point through which Satan enters the home.

GUESS WHO HAS BEEN FATHERING
OUR CHILDREN

Children growing up in such environments often suffer from a lack of self-worth, which has been proved to be a significant factor in cases of drug and alcohol abuse, as well as violent criminal activity, teenage pregnancy and under-achievement in schools.

YOU MAY NOT BE ABLE TO CHANGE YOUR ANCESTORS, BUT YOU CAN CERTAINLY DO SOMETHING ABOUT YOUR DESCENDANTS.

A certain man who was a pastor as well as a father lived in a community in an inner-city neighbourhood in America, where most of the children were either taking drugs or selling them. It grieved him to such a degree that he actively prayed to God to see what should be done. God showed the pastor that he had been upset about the success of the drug-pushers' efforts over the efforts of the church and parents in the community to eliminate the drugs. What he ought to have been more interested in was isolating and eliminating the root of the problem.

The pastor was driven to actually approach the drug-pushers directly and boldly demand to know why they were so successful in peddling their drugs and destroying the community. The response was sinister but simple: 'We are always here, you are never there.' The children are on the streets daily, exposed to everything. Their parents are at work daily, leaving the children open to all manners of undesirable activities and people. The push-ers moved in on their emotionally starved prey, hanging out with them, playing basketball with them, mentoring them and acting as role models.

SHAPING OUR CHILDREN'S DESTINY

If you fail to raise your own child, society will perform the task for you, but usually to your detriment. You may not be able to change your ancestors, but you can certainly do something about your descendants. Nurturing children can be likened to sitting at a stool and moulding clay images. The way the material is treated and how it is handled will determine the result. We can take lessons in helping to form our children from looking at the successes as well as the failings of our experiences in growing up.

The life-stages of a child can be divided into a number of phases:

The infancy stage covers the first twelve months of a child's life; between the ages of one and three the child experiences *toddler-hood*. Three to five-year-olds are known as *'pre-schoolers';* ages five to twelve are the described as the *school years;* and years thirteen to twenty cover *adolescence.*

THE RESPONSE WAS SINISTER BUT SIMPLE: 'WE ARE ALWAYS HERE, YOU ARE NEVER THERE.'

All the stages are important but the first five to seven years are critical in the child's development. Around age five, when children are entering school they are exposed to a whole new world. Whatever methods were employed in moulding the child before that age will influence how the child responds to society and its influences.

A) Infancy

During *infancy*, a child is attached to its primary caregiver. This is the phase in which a child's security in life is formed. Trust is being built at this time and their assurance that life is 'good' is being developed. People who do not trust others, who are afraid in life and feel insecure, may have had a negative experience during this phase of our development.

The primary need of a child in this phase is nourishment. All babies seem to do is sleep, eat and demand a nappy change! There is a lot more going on, physically, psychologically and emotionally, though. When babies require a need to be met, their primary source of communication is crying. When parents do not respond adequately, what the child comes to believe is that nobody cares.

During a study of children, a comparative investigation with the young of some other mammals (animals who suckle their young with milk), produced interesting results. It was found that the fat and protein content in the milk of a mother rabbit is highly concentrated. When rabbits breastfeed, another feed is not needed for a further twenty-four hours. The tree shrew needs only to feed her young every forty-eight hours. The milk of human beings was analysed and was found to be quite 'weak' in comparison.

BABIES NEED MORE THAN MILK

It would seem alarming at first, but it is a marvel when one realises the effects of having to feed human babies on a much more frequent basis. God has deliberately designed us in such a way that our children need to be fed every few hours. This is because He wants us to form strong bonds with our children. The child needs a regular, close emotional embrace, which ensures that he or she feels warm, safe and special. Stronger, more concentrated milk from the mother would need to be supplied to the child at less regular intervals, reducing the effects of the nurturing function. In most cases, breast-fed babies are the best-fed babies.

B) Toddler-hood

The second stage in life, *toddler-hood*, is the phase when children begin to develop their sense of 'self'. During infancy, the child is totally dependent upon the parents. The child and its mother can almost be regarded as one individual unit. There is little separation between the mother's body and the child's own because of breast-feeding and because of the constant need to be held. By contrast, during its second phase the child becomes less dependent, both physically and emotionally. Physically, because he or she is crawling around, crawling away and learning to walk, no longer needing the parents to carry them everywhere. Emotionally, because the child begins to build and appreciate relationships with other people.

A child should be encouraged to explore life during this stage within gentle, loving boundaries. Too much restriction at this age can lead to a lack of self-confidence. Toddlers like playing a kind of game with their parents, to test their limits. You will find that a lot of them go through a phase where they suddenly make off into the distance, but keep looking back to see the parents' response before they go further. This is one way that they can see how far they can go, before the parents put their foot down and become serious or worried.

These children want their independence, yet they also need to be given a sense of security and the knowledge that the parent is always there in the background to care for them and to come to their rescue. Children who have negative experiences during this phase have difficulty overcoming a fear of failure later in life. They do not get the opportunity to safely develop a sense of adventure, and so don't feel that adventure is a safe thing. It may affect their ability to take risks or to try something new. There may appear to be too much uncertainty in the world and this type of person always needs to perceive a safety net of some description.

The *toddler-hood* stage is also when the child begins to develop a sense of self-worth. If this phase is not handled with care, a child can develop a low self-esteem and a lack of self-confidence.

B) Preschool stage

The next stage is the *pre-school* stage. This is between the ages of three and five years old. It is a stage where sexual identities begin to form. This is the age where children begin to take an interest in their genitalia. A curiosity begins to develop regarding the parts of the body, and the child will begin to notice the differences between his body parts and those of other people he sees. He or she will recognise whether his body is more like daddy's or mummy's and align with other boys or girls accordingly. Care should be taken at this phase not to give the child the image that there is something 'naughty', 'sinister' or 'bad' about their genitalia, even though it would be preferable not to openly discuss them in public!

Their sexual identity begins to form, and children start imagining what they are going to be when they 'grow-up'. Role modelling begins at this stage. In the past, boys would have picked up on stereotypical occupations, saying that they want to be a policeman or a fire-fighter. Girls would sometimes say they want to be a nurse. They begin to see a person after whom they would like to model themselves.

This is also the stage where children have the beginnings of an appreciation of marriage. They can see a sexual difference and recognise a difference in the role of

their father and how it differs from the role of their
mother. This is the stage where they need to see their
parents demonstrating affection towards each other. He
or she will notice how the parents speak to themselves
and how well they respect each other. The opinion is
being formed here as to whether or not marriage is a
good thing. When children grow up, the way they relate
to their spouse will often be based upon, or at least
influenced by, what they saw of their parents' marriage
during this important phase.

Girls particularly need to receive affirmation that they
are valued, valuable and fully acceptable. If a girl goes
through difficulties during this phase, it damages her
sexuality in later life. She may never become fully mature as a woman. If she has trouble at this stage and goes
on to become a mother herself, she may overcompensate
for the inadequacies suffered by clinging on to her children for validation, particularly her boys, and seriously
impede their own development.

BEGINNING OF GENDER CONFUSION

She will possibly derive some sort of emotional succour
from her sons, pouring an unhealthy amount of emotion
out onto them and make certain that they remain
'mummy's boys' well into their pre-school years. Problems naturally occur when the child starts resenting the
interaction that he witnesses between his mother and her
husband. He will feel an unnatural jealousy because the
mother has nurtured an 'Oedipal Complex' in her son.

Even if physical incest does not develop, emotional incest does and it is this type of environment that engenders and breeds the spirit of homosexuality.

Equally, if the mother dies, leaves the home or abandons her daughter in her very early years leaving the daughter to be raised by an austere, dominant, critical father, it will leave her craving for the love of a mother and she will end up seeking it in another woman. All she is usually looking for is the embrace of an absent mother, but when she ends up embracing a woman too long, it will lead to other things. The daughter will have become hardened by having to counteract the harshness of an abrasive father and will exhibit tough, aggressive behaviour unusual in a female. She has had to become tough to deal with daddy, and this can lead to lesbianism.

If mothers do not allow their children to fully explore and develop their own sense of 'self' at the toddler stage, when they reach adolescence they will not have truly gained the independence that their peers manage to attain. They remain insecure, exhibit anti-social behaviour and the cycle therefore continues with their own offspring. The sad thing is that many parents act this way without considering the long-term damage that they are causing, both to their children and to the next generation as a whole.

D) School Years

The next stage in life is the school years. This is the time of academic ability, the time when children's skills, special talents and gifts need to be developed. Although this is an important phase, the previous years are much more formative, therefore most of the work needs to be concentrated on these years to ensure that the child has a productive future.

E) *Adolescence*

Adolescence is the stage in life when one wants to develop significance for oneself. One begins seeking the purpose of life as well as one's own purpose in life. Some of us may have had a great childhood, but later on in life we became estranged from our parents. Maybe we were sent to a boarding school, or sent away from home to live with relatives. I still remember my first day at boarding school. When I encountered the menacing older boys, I was gripped with a sense of fear and my first thought was 'where are my parents?' It is one point in life where one feels fragile, alone and vulnerable. I felt as though life is a scary place to be and I knew that I would now have to chart my own course. It is all well and good to know that on one level, but the truth is, I was afraid; afraid of having to face each day alone, with all the tough new challenges ahead of me — facing bullies, facing responsibilities, facing life. You spend large portions of each day wondering 'where is everybody?'

This is the stage in life where definitions are made, a sense of 'who you are'. Many of us did not have a string of commendable mentors whom we could emulate or who could tell us how to be an adult, how a man ought to be, what a real woman does, how a woman should be treated and so on. We end up learning such things from magazines, television, influential friends and acquaintances, all of whom have become our surrogate parents.

At this stage, parents need to put the 'extra' unto the 'ordinary' to develop 'extraordinary' children. Some of these 'extras' include the following:

Develop A Sharp Purpose

One develops a sharp purpose firstly through recognising, even before the child is born, that one has just been granted custody of a potential giant. The first steps a parent ought to take should be to seek guidance from God as to the nature of the child's destiny, and then to name, nurture and groom him or her accordingly.

Develop A Family Mission Statement

It is good practice to have a mission statement that describes and determines that in which you and your family believe, that for which you and your household stand united, and that to which you and your family adhere. The mission statement for our church indicates that we are committed to developing leaders who will influence society. The mission statement for my home is that we are a home built on the solid Rock who is Christ. Christian values are the very foundations of our house. We welcome the hurting and broken into a place of healing, empowerment and illumination. It is a place where we stand for morality and nurture greatness.

A new child coming into your home can be groomed to conform to a certain code of conduct, appreciating that when he or she does something that is off the mark, they will be reminded that such behaviour is not in line with your mission statement.

Develop a Keen Mind

When my child was born I read many of the child development books and bought heaps of stimulating material with various colours and interesting shapes. I also bought a lot of the groceries that were said to stimulate mental growth. Some people may have said that I went a bit over the top, but to me it was worth it because something appeared to be working. They are both quite intelligent, curious and active children.

It is important that children be exposed to many different stimuli and experiences. When a child is born his brain may appear to be a little blob, but within the first few years of life it will grow phenomenally. The more experiences a child has, the more connectivity there will be between his or her nerve cells. A child's brain can be compared to a computer. Just as with a computer, good results can only be obtained from it if first-class software has been programmed in. If you only let garbage go in, you will only ever get garbage out.

Develop Your Child's Gift

Every child is uniquely gifted. Some parents may wonder whether this is really true of their child, especially given the report cards he or she sometimes brings home from school. This should not be viewed as an indication of the child's potential, because without exception, all children have been created with a special gift inside them. You may not yet have seen any sign of a gift, and this might even have more to do with you than it has to do with the child. His or her strong point may not be reading, writing or arithmetic but he or she may have an outstanding physical ability. If you try to force your child to become an aeronautical engineer when there is a world-class football player inside him, you have destroyed his life. Whether it is a physical, mental or musical ability that has been placed in your child, as the child grows in the right climate that gift will begin to blossom.

DO NOT JUST DREAM ABOUT THE GOOD DAYS AHEAD. START TO PLANT THE RIGHT SEEDS THAT WILL PRODUCE YOUR EXPECTED FUTURE.

You need to model the behaviour that you would like to see reflected in your child. In other words, lead by example. My son likes to pick up books and pretend to read them. He cannot read yet, but he sees his parents reading quite a bit and wants so much to be in on the act! Parents who do not spend much time reading should not be surprised or even cross when their children bring home poor reports from school regarding reading progress.

Develop Your Child's Skills

As well as his or her gift, it is important that a child's skills also receive adequate training. Leadership skills are important from an early age. If developed correctly, it will not matter whether your child has been elected the official leader in a certain situation, their natural leadership skills will shine through and they will be the ones to influence other people, rather than it being the other way around.

Social skills need to be taught to our children from a young age. These are issues that many of our parents generation did not really feel the need to pass on, presuming perhaps that we would pick them up at some point in life. We need to teach our young such things as how to build relationships or how to comport themselves in public. How to greet people: posture, grace, presence and so on. How to portray the right image, exude confidence and command respect.

My son loves to sing Christian songs and songs about Jesus, even in school. His teacher recently told me that she had noticed how much he loves Bible stories because he brings his books to school and tells the other children all about them. One day quite recently my son proudly announced, 'Daddy, I told my friends in school how much I love Jesus. I told them!' He was really beaming from ear to ear, so pleased with himself that all I could say to that was, 'Good boy, you tell them again tomorrow!'

Do not just dream about the good days ahead. Start to plant the right seeds that will produce your expected future. The law of compound interest and the law of sowing and reaping will work in your favour. Start to work while it is day because the future is truly in your hands.

References:

Pytches, Mary. Yesterday's Child (Healing Present Problems By Understanding the Past), *London, Hodder & Stoughton, 1990.*

Smith, P.K. et al. Understanding Children's Development, *Oxford, Blackwell, 1998.*

Haggard, Ted et al. Confident Parents, Exceptional Teens, *Michigan, Zondervan Publishing House, 1999.*

Elmore, Tim. Nurturing the Leader Within Your Child, *Nashville, Thomas Nelson Publishers, 2001.*

Conclusion:

WHOSE MIRROR ARE YOU LOOKING INTO?

It is quite evident from the previous chapters that we have an enemy who is striving relentlessly to destroy the way we see ourselves. If you want to rob a man of his power and his destiny, tell him a lie — that he is power-less — or focus his energies and attention on his weak-nesses. A lion who has from birth been brainwashed into believing that he is a mouse will be an impotent wimp lacking both in boldness and in bite. This clearly illustrates Satan's chief strategy, trying to make us see ourselves in the lowliest possible light. Don't believe the lie; believe your mirror image.

'Anyone who listens to the word but does not do what it says is like a man who looks at his face in a mirror and, after looking at himself, goes away and immediately forgets what he looks like.' (James 1:23-25)

The greatest remedy against a lie is the plain truth. If you have been told that all the money you had in the bank has been stolen or spent, this will naturally cause serious anxiety. However, the anxiety could quickly be remedied if you were shown your true bank statement — in other words, if you were shown the *real* state of things. This act would restore a calmness and security that sleeping pills could never give. The only antidote for a lie is the truth.

EVE BELIEVED A LIE

Never underestimate the power of the devil to deceive. He hijacked the destiny of the entire human race through deceit. Eve did not have her facts right, ignored God's Word and suffered as a consequence.

> IF YOU WANT TO ROB A MAN
> OF HIS POWER AND HIS DESTINY,
> TELL HIM A LIE — THAT HE IS
> POWERLESS — OR FOCUS HIS
> ENERGIES AND ATTENTION ON
> HIS WEAKNESSES.

Satan has, for many years, tried to destroy our personality. Yet still his most lethal weapon against us is to destroy both the way we perceive ourselves and the things we believe about ourselves.

'"You will not surely die," the serpent said to the woman. "For God knows that when you eat

of it your eyes will be opened and you will be like God, knowing good and evil.'" (Genesis 3:4-5).

He succeeded in getting Eve to believe that she was not quite 'up to scratch'. He gave her the feeling that she really was not what God had created her to be. That she needed a little touch-up to look normal, possibly a little liposuction, maybe a face-lift, get some silicon implanted and perhaps start taking some diet pills! He made her believe that God had made her somehow imperfect or incomplete, so some further action would need to be taken on her part to make her 'perfect'.

THE GREATEST REMEDY AGAINST A LIE IS THE PLAIN TRUTH.

Eve lost her place, position and purpose in life because she refused to continually present the truth of her real identity before her mind; that God had made her and Adam in His image and likeness and therefore they were already like God. They did not need to eat the fruit of the tree of knowledge of good and evil to become like Him. All Satan did to conquer that woman was to introduce a little 'self-doubt' in the form of suggestive thought, and that was when the first seeds of insecurity were sown.

A CLOSER LOOK IN THE MIRROR

The only way you can know true security and draw strength from your real identity is by continually beholding God's true image of you as set out in the Holy Bible. God made you in His true image and likeness. There is much more to you than the person you think yourself to be. This is the hidden truth that your own mirror cannot reveal and no doctor is able to heal.

You are a unique creation, created by the finest Designer for a specific purpose. You are beautiful for your situation, the Designer's masterpiece. Believe in the God who believes in you.

MY FATHER'S WORD
(*The Story of an Unwanted Child*)

D r Sola Fola-Alade was the very last of my five children, all from my late wife Yemi. He was simply one child
too many for me, as we had closed shop after four (two
girls and two boys). But due to my 'carelessness' and my
wife's miscalculation, a Sola-foetus came! When Yemi told
me, she saw my disappointment. We agreed to abort the
pregnancy, against her doctor's advice. However, as hard
as we tried to snuff him out, he only kept growing in the
womb; until he stormed out seven weeks too early, nearly
killing her at birth. She died a few years later.

A RADICAL CHANGE

On 21 March 1990 he rang me in great excitement from
medical school. 'I am a mature man now!', he declared.
'Are you sure you are feeling all right?' I asked. He re-
plied, 'Yes! I am now a full man, a child of God who has
given his life to Jesus.' I was shocked, dazed and confused.
I could not see what I had done wrong. We argued – neither of us giving way – until we reached a point where I
told him, 'I pay your fees for medical studies, not for Bible
study.' His response was, 'Stop my fees and I will stop

your medicine, but I'll hold on to my Bible.' I never thought my beloved last son could stand up to me so brazenly! I am not the type of person who prays seriously, unless I am in serious trouble: but now I went down on my knees for a long prayer session. But God warned me: 'Handle this matter with care, or lose this child of God.'

FROM MEDICINE TO MINISTRY

I urged Sola to complete his medical studies. 'If you fail to become a doctor, you'll be called a failure, a drop-out and a quitter. But any audience will listen more to a Doctor-Pastor, who can heal both the body and the soul!' God did hear my prayers, just as Sola heard my sermon. He practised medicine for a few years and at the same time worked as a part-time pastor. Then God Himself sent him to London for full-ministering unto the Lord. And now he is married, has gotten me two grandsons and he leads a very dynamic life-changing church. All I can say is: 'To God be the glory, great things He has done!'

AN UNUSUAL BOY

Sola has always demonstrated a creative and entrepreneurial spirit. At the age of 9 he wrote a little book that stunned me, his school teachers and friends. He was curious, precocious, and a pest to many in his insatiable quest for knowledge. The response of his impatient teachers to his many questions was merely to tell him to be quiet.

GOD DID THE IMPOSSIBLE

As a single parent, a widower now for twenty-seven years, I thank God for a motherless child like Sola, who has had to be dependent mainly on me as mother as well as father.

My friends keep telling me of the positive influence Sola has been on their children and themselves, both in London and Nigeria. I am simply proud of him. He is now the crown of my family and the best-known of us at home and abroad. That, to me, is a miracle.

He used to read quickly and speak quickly with a little stammer. Now he speaks with such clarity and eloquence. That makes me appreciate the grace of God upon His life even more.

Last July, in his London flat, I read his last book in five hours. It impressed and inspired me. I told him and his wife that my unwanted son's book has (at last) inspired me to *Discover My Hidden Treasures* and to write my own book soon, with God's help.

And now, as my Doctor, Teacher and Pastor, it is my honour and pleasure to toast my miracle son Sola, '*my 'once-unwanted' son, in whom I am well pleased'*. May your children too, grow to be greater than you in your lifetime.

Chief Isaac Fola-Alade, OFR, FINA, RIBA
(Chartered Architect & Consultant)

THE PHYSICIAN

WHO IS HE?

The best doctors are not necessarily those with the most letters after their names, nor are they the ones who have done the most research. The greatest doctors are those who have been patients themselves, and know what it feels like to have an illness or undergo surgery. Those physicians are able to be more sensitive to their patients' needs. Their approach to their patients will be more sympathetic, and will be informed by the empathy of their heart rather than merely the information in their head.

Jesus Christ is the greatest physician who ever walked the face of the earth, because even though He was God, He thought it necessary to take on the form and frailties of man in order to understand man's experience and thus deliver him from the bondage of sinful flesh. *'We do not have a high priest who is unable to sympathise with our weaknesses, but we have one who has been tempted in every way, just as we are — yet was without sin'* (Hebrews 4: 15).

WHAT DOES HE DO?

If you have any unresolved issues, challenges or secret pain in your life, or you need someone to walk with you through this dark or tortuous life, place your life in the hands of the Greatest Physician. If you need Him to come into your life, to change it for ever and lead you to a place of eternal bliss with God, say this prayer with me and you will experience the changing power of the Great Physician.

THE PRAYER

Dear Jesus, I am sorry for my sins and I ask You to please forgive me now, as I turn away from everything that I know is wrong. Thank You that You died for my sins on the cross and that You rose again on the third day, so that I can live a new victorious life. Please forgive my sins, cleanse my heart and come into my life. I also ask that You give me the gift of your Holy Spirit, who will heal me and teach me about You and Your plans for my life. Thank You for accepting me as Your child.

Dr Sola Fola Alade *trained as a medical doctor and now* pastors **Trinity Chapel**, *a growing and dynamic church he planted with 6 people in 1996. He attended the International Bible Institute of London, Kensington Temple and later went on to pursue an MBA at the East London Business School (University of East London).*

Sola has a particular passion and anointing to raise Christians as leaders in the market place and prepare them for positions of influence in society. He is the CEO of **The Spearhead Group**, *a human resource development consultancy for career and business professionals. He is married to Abimbola and they together have two sons, Toni and Tola.*

If this book has impacted you,

please write to the author at:

info@developingleaders.net

VISION MEDIA COMMUNICATIONS
Present

LIVING ON THE CUTTING EDGE

(30 one-minute, motivational messages on CD)

The attainment of success or failure in life is dependent on the astuteness of your spirit, the ability of your mind and the agility of your body. It takes a person who has developed these three parts of their being to utilise and maximise the many opportunities life will present, more so as these opportunities usually present themselves in the form of challenges.

These messages by **Dr Sola Fola-Alade** will inspire you towards success and lasting achievement.

For your copy:
info@developingleaders.net

VISION MEDIA COMMUNICATIONS
Present
DISCOVER YOUR HIDDEN TREASURES
By Dr Sola Fola-Alade

This book will help you:

Discover the unique gifts God has placed in you.
Turn your hidden resources into real wealth.
Understand intellectual property and how to
take advantage of the new economy.
Discern and maximise the different seasons of your life.
Build enduring generational wealth.

For your copy:
info@developingleaders.net